Problem
of Good

11/22/2015

Happy Birth[day]
one of our
friends!
Lord bless
you w[ith]
many birth keep in the
future. Our Love,
Cheryl & Dennis

to

The Problem of Good

When the World Seems Fine without God

Edited by D. Marion Clark

P&R
PUBLISHING
P.O. BOX 817 • PHILLIPSBURG • NEW JERSEY 08865-0817

ISBN: 978-1-59638-870-3 (pbk)
ISBN: 978-1-59638-871-0 (ePub)
ISBN: 978-1-59638-872-7 (Mobi)

Printed in the United States of America

Library of Congress Control Number: 2014943269

To my three greatest common grace blessings:
my wife, Ginger, and daughters, Sarah and Jean.

Contents

Foreword   ix
Philip G. Ryken

Acknowledgments   xiii

Introduction: The Problem of Good   xv
D. Marion Clark

Part One: An Exposition of the Doctrine of Common Grace

1. Restraining Sin and Wrath   3
   Steven J. Lawson

2. My Father's World: The Good Gifts of Common Grace   23
   Sean Michael Lucas

Part Two: Application of Common Grace for Worship and Life

3. Worshiping and Glorifying the Creator and Provider   39
   D. Marion Clark

4. Sharing the Gospel in Light of Common Grace   55
   John Leonard

5. Common Grace and Loving Your Neighbor   71
   Ruth Naomi Floyd

CONTENTS

6. How Should We Then Live in the World?   87
    David Skeel

7. How May We Learn from the World?   103
    Gene Edward Veith

8. Hardwired for Pleasure   121
    Paul David Tripp

9. The "Good" Neighbor   135
    D. Marion Clark

    Conclusion: The Limits of Common Grace   149
    D. Marion Clark

    Notes   161

    Contributors   165

Foreword

Philip G. Ryken

THE "PROBLEM OF EVIL" poses a serious challenge to faith, and it has occupied the minds of the best thinkers and theologians for millennia—at least since the time of Job. If God is good, then why do bad things happen in his good creation, including the bad things that happen to good people?

This is a difficult question, to be sure. What is not always recognized, however, is that the "problem of good" is every bit as challenging for people who do not believe in God or are unsure what to believe. If there is no God, then the material universe is the only ultimate reality. There is no soul; there is only matter. In that case, how can we explain the transcendent joy that rises in the human heart when a mother caresses her baby's cheek, or when an orchestra plays the triumphant chords at the climax of a Beethoven symphony, or when a red dawn breaks over the far horizon, or when lovers are reunited after being separated by war? Are wonder and awe spiritual realities, or are they nothing more than chemical reactions in the brain? Apart from the existence of God, what basis do we have for saying that some things are truly good?

Christians face a different struggle with good (and evil). It is easy enough for us to explain the existence of good: it is a gift from God. We may even be able to begin to explain the existence of evil: it is the consequence of sin. But still we struggle to explain why good things happen to bad people. We live in a moral universe, in which sin brings people under the judgment of a holy God. So why do so many sinners—including people who reject God outright—receive so many divine blessings? And why does God allow so many good things to happen in the world through the actions of people who do not serve him as well as through people who do?

The biblical doctrine that helps us answer these complex questions is "common grace"—common in the sense that it is universal. God has not given all his gifts or all his grace only to Christians. On the contrary, "The LORD is good to all, and his mercy is over all that he has made" (Ps. 145:9). Or again, "Every good gift and every perfect gift is from above" (James 1:17). This evidently includes the gifts that God gives to people who do not claim to follow Christ as well as to the people who do follow Christ. As James Davison Hunter wrote in his influential book *To Change the World*, "People of every creed and no creed have talents and abilities, possess knowledge, wisdom, and inventiveness, and hold standards of goodness, truth, justice, morality, and beauty that are, in relative degree, in harmony with God's will and purposes."[1]

This means that God accomplishes his gracious purpose in the world through non-Christians as well as Christians. Their work can bring glory to God, even when that is not their explicit intent. So a man like Wolfgang Amadeus Mozart (who at least for most of his life was not a practicing Christian) brought as much glory to God through his music as a man like Johann Sebastian Bach (who signed many of his compositions with the letters "sDg," meaning "to God alone be the glory"). This is not to deny the profound difference between the heart motivation of a writer or composer who wants to honor God and the heart motivation of a person who doesn't. Their motivations may well affect the quality of their work in tangible as well as intangible ways. And yet, by the grace of God, the gifts of the unbeliever still honor the God who gave them.

Admittedly, common grace is not saving grace, and the blessings that come with creation fall short of full redemption—they will not bring anyone into eternal life. Common grace relates to life in the present world, with or without a loving relationship with God through Jesus Christ. Only saving grace brings people into a personal friendship with the living God that lasts forever. Thus it is important to recognize the limitations as well as the implications of common grace.

These principles are not nearly as well understood as they ought to be. Theologians have done comparatively little work in analyzing and explaining the doctrine of common grace. And many lay people are unfamiliar with the doctrine at all, despite its profound relevance for daily life.

We may all be grateful, therefore, that Marion Clark and his friends from ministry and other walks of life have written this book. Pastor Clark has dedicated his life to explaining biblical truth in clear, practical ways and to solving spiritual problems in the life of the church. He does all of that here in *The Problem of Good*. There is no other book like it—nothing that offers a basic overview and complete introduction to the doctrine of common grace. As a result, people who read this book will be uncommonly prepared to think through complex problems and to live out their faith in the church and in the world.

Acknowledgments

THE SEED FOR THIS BOOK PROJECT was planted when I asked Phil Ryken (at that time Senior Minister of Tenth Presbyterian Church) to recommend a book on common grace for my summer reading. Surprisingly, he was stymied. We agreed that someone ought to write such a book. A number of years later a sabbatical gave me opportunity for further study and the planning of this book. Thanks go to Lydia Brownback for the suggestion of a collaboration with other writers. I am thankful for all the contributors, who understood the significance of the subject and were willing to use their talents for such a work. The editors at P&R grasped the concept of what I wanted to accomplish and have guided an idea to production.

Readers wanting to read further will find resources in the endnotes, but several works were most helpful to me. There is the three-volume work on common grace by the Dutch theologian Abraham Kuyper. His *Common Grace*[1] is the one comprehensive treatment of the doctrine, but it has not been available in English. A translation project is underway and the full work should be completed in the near future. I benefited from the initial offering of that project, *Wisdom and Wonder: Common Grace in Science and Art.*[2] All theologians addressing the subject subsequently had to interact with Kuyper. Of those writers, I have been helped by Herman Bavinck's "Calvin and Common Grace,"[3] Cornelius Van Til's *Common Grace and the Gospel,*[4] and John Murray's "Common Grace" from *Collected Writings of John Murray, Vol. 2: Systematic Theology.*[5]

Social commentator Ken Myers of Mars Hill Audio wrote a helpful piece entitled "Christianity, Culture, and Common Grace."[6] Richard Mouw published a helpful book called *He Shines in All That's Fair: Culture and Common Grace*.[7] He expressed hope of reviving discussion of the doctrine. *The Problem of Good* is a modest attempt to do the same.

The Problem of Good

D. Marion Clark

THE PROBLEM OF GOOD for many Christians is twofold.
The first is how to make sense of the "good" found in the unregenerate. Consider this poem.

> She walks in beauty, like the night
> Of cloudless climes and starry skies;
> And all that's best of dark and bright
> Meet in her aspect and her eyes:
> Thus mellowed to that tender light
> Which heaven to gaudy day denies.
>
> One shade the more, one ray the less,
> Had half impaired the nameless grace
> Which waves in every raven tress,
> Or softly lightens o'er her face;
> Where thoughts serenely sweet express
> How pure, how dear, their dwelling-place.
>
> And on that cheek, and o'er that brow,
> So soft, so calm, yet eloquent,
> The smiles that win, the tints that glow,
> But tell of days in goodness spent,
> A mind at peace with all below,
> A heart whose love is innocent![1]

This beautiful, tender poem was written by a man whose character provided the model for Count Dracula. He was described by one woman as "mad, bad, and dangerous to know," an accurate description that both women and men would learn after his seductions. He was Lord Byron. How did such a cad write so beautiful a poem, one that captures inner moral beauty?

Or take another example, this time of a great tune composer and arranger of hymns. One of the best-regarded hymns is "For All the Saints." The words are moving.

> But lo! there breaks a yet more glorious day;
> The saints triumphant rise in bright array;
> The King of Glory passes on his way.
> Alleluia! Alleluia!
>
> From earth's wide bounds, from ocean's farthest coast,
> Through gates of pearl streams in the countless host,
> Singing to Father, Son, and Holy Ghost,
> Alleluia! Alleluia![2]

They are all the more moving when sung to the tune "Sine Nomine," composed by Ralph Vaughan Williams, notable for his church music. And yet Williams did not believe in this King of Glory. He was an agnostic if not an atheist. How could a composer whose heart was not bent toward the King of Glory produce music that leads the King's disciples into moving worship?

This is the problem of good. We live in a world that is at odds with its Creator and whose human creatures are in rebellion against their Ruler, and yet this same world has produced beautiful, truth-filled writings, music, and concepts that have enriched our appreciation of and devotion to the Creator and Ruler whom we do acknowledge, serve, and worship. How can this be? How can unregenerate men and women understand so much about the God they deny, or use their gifts to express truth about him? How can persons who are "darkened in their understanding, alienated from the life of God because of the ignorance that is in them, due to their hardness of heart" (Eph. 4:18) nevertheless discover, contemplate, teach, express, and produce works that exemplify truth, beauty, and insight about God, his creation, his works, and even his redemptive work?

Or perhaps more perplexing and troubling, how can unregenerate individuals whose hearts of stone have not been replaced with hearts of flesh by the Holy Spirit (see Ezek. 36:26) still live moral, compassionate lives that are similar, if not superior, to those of regenerate followers of Christ? All of us who follow Christ can point to some neighbor who seems to be naturally hospitable, loving, even devoted to worshiping God, but who does not know God in Christ. How can this be? Scripture says this about the unregenerate:

> None is righteous, no, not one;
>> no one understands;
>> no one seeks for God.
> All have turned aside; together they have become worthless;
>> no one does good,
>> not even one. (Rom. 3:10–12)

But we can see good in most of our unregenerate neighbors, and there are neighbors who outdo us in doing good. How can that be?

This—the good, truth, and beauty that confront us from our unregenerate neighbors of the rebellious world—is what shakes the faith of many Christians even more than the problem of evil. The fall of Adam and Eve teaches us to understand that the world is filled with evil and that bad things will happen even to regenerate followers of Christ. Bad stuff happens. But why does good stuff happen, not merely *to* the unregenerate but even *through* them?

How necessary is the gospel to make bad people good? How necessary is the regenerating work of the Holy Spirit to bring light and truth into the human heart? And if a measure of good and truth can be acknowledged to exist in the unregenerate, then we are led eventually to ask the next question: how can God justly deny them entry into his heavenly kingdom, much less condemn them to hell?

It is this train of thought that has led some Christians to compromise the gospel faith, if not to abandon it altogether. Grappling with the problem of good challenges, in particular, Christians who have grown up immersed in Christian culture. They have been raised in Christian homes, attended Christian schools, and worshiped in biblically based churches. Then they go off to a secular college or join the secular workforce or in some other way come into real-life contact with the so-called pagan world. Prepared for the evil in the world, they are tripped up by the good they find. Instead of darkened minds, they find minds that seem more enlightened than theirs; instead of calloused hearts, they find warm hearts; instead of self-centered egos, they find people devoted to justice and serving the needy. And none of these people follow Christ, unless it's in a way that regards him as a moral teacher.

Are we Christians, then, the ones who got it all wrong? Were we taught wrong by our churches and teachers? Is the gospel wrong, or were we maybe taught a defective view of the gospel? What if the story of the prodigal son was not the right perspective? What if the elder brother had visited his younger brother and found that his brother was actually doing well and living among good, though pagan, neighbors?

That is problem one. Then there is problem two: can Christians benefit from the contributions of the unregenerate, and if so, how? We have no difficulty accepting the contributions of unbelieving engineers, doctors, and plumbers. What do we do with unbelieving philosophers, sociologists, and psychologists? What do we do with the intellectual contributions in all fields? A suspicion of the unregenerate has led many Christians to a self-quarantine from the world and their neighbors, fearful that contact will infect their minds and souls with what is false and immoral. Indeed, the suspicion leads them to reject almost everything that the unregenerate present, presuming that nothing they see and present can be in keeping with Scripture.

This may be a valid concern, but the perspective presumes that God cannot and will not work in and through his creatures unless they are redeemed. Is it true that God can operate only through the redeemed? Calvin reflected on this subject in his *Institutes of the Christian Religion*:

> Whenever we come upon these matters in secular writers, let that admirable light of truth shining in them teach us that the mind of man though fallen and perverted from its wholeness, is nevertheless clothed and ornamented with God's excellent gifts. If we regard the Spirit of God as the sole fountain of truth, we shall neither reject the truth itself, nor despise it wherever it shall appear, unless we wish to dishonor the Spirit of God. For by holding the gifts of the Spirit in slight esteem, we contemn and reproach the Spirit himself. What then? Shall we deny that the truth shone upon the ancient jurists who established civic order and discipline with such great equity? Shall we say that the philosophers were blind in their fine observation and artful description of nature? Shall we say that those men were devoid of understanding who conceived the art of disputation and taught us to speak reasonably? Shall we say that they are insane who developed medicine, devoting their labor to our benefit? What shall we say of all the mathematical sciences? Shall we consider them the ravings of madmen? No, we cannot read the writings of the ancients on these subjects without great admiration. We marvel at them because we are compelled to recognize how preeminent they are. But shall we count anything praiseworthy or noble without recognizing at the same time that it comes from God? Let us be ashamed of such ingratitude, into which not even the pagan poets fell, for they confessed that the gods had invented philosophy, laws, and all useful arts. Those men whom Scripture [1 Cor. 2:14] calls "natural men" were, indeed, sharp and penetrating in their investigation of inferior things. Let us, accordingly, learn

> by their example how many gifts the Lord left to human nature even after it was despoiled of its true good.[3]

As Calvin noted, it is irrefutable that the unregenerate mind is "clothed and ornamented with God's excellent gifts." Even so, Calvin also notes limits to such a mind.

> But lest anyone think a man truly blessed when he is credited with possessing great power to comprehend truth under the elements of this world [cf. Col. 2:8], we should at once add that all this capacity to understand, with the understanding that follows upon it, is an unstable and transitory thing in God's sight, when a solid foundation of truth does not underlie it.[4]

So then, what may we trust that comes from the intellect of the unregenerate mind? What may we enjoy that comes from the creativity and skill of the defiled heart? May we or may we not borrow from and even take delight in the unregenerate world?

This book addresses both of those problems through an explication of the doctrine of common grace. The doctrine is often cited in fleeting reference but is rarely expounded. When understood, it is the key that opens the door to much understanding. How do we regard our neighbors? How should we be involved in the world? Common grace explains. And it adds to our ability to worship and serve God in ways that we may not have given thought to.

What is common grace? John Murray gives the most succinct definition: "Every favor of whatever kind or degree, falling short of salvation, which this undeserving and sin–cursed world enjoys at the hand of God."[5] As Jesus put it, God the Father "makes his sun rise on the evil and on the good, and sends rain on the just and on the unjust" (Matt. 5:45).

Why would God show such favor and give good gifts to the evil and the unjust? In his Sermon on the Mount message, from which the above verse is taken, Jesus introduces the idea in the context of loving one's enemy. He presents his Father as the model for such love, which is displayed through these common grace gifts. In Luke's gospel, Jesus specifically says that God is "kind to the ungrateful and the evil" and that we are to be so merciful "even as your Father is merciful" (Luke 6:35–36).

The remainder of this book will present a fuller definition and application of common grace. The first two chapters present the biblical teaching about the doctrine, specifically its role in restraining sin and in bestowing good gifts. Steven Lawson will address the ways in which God restrains sin, the decay of his image, and evil as well as how God restrains his own wrath. Sean Lucas then explains how God does not merely restrain sin in man but induces a measure of good so that men and women act with a conscience, abide by a code of conduct, and even love their neighbors. He also demonstrates how God bestows good gifts outwardly—the blessings of the natural world—and inwardly—the blessings of intellect and creativity.

We will then consider the application of common grace. How should an understanding of common grace affect the way we worship and live out our faith before the world? I will address specifically how the knowledge of common grace impacts our worship. John Leonard then explores how an understanding of common grace influences the way we witness for the gospel. And Ruth Floyd considers what common grace has to say to us about loving our neighbors.

What then does the doctrine teach us about living in the world? David Skeel deliberates that specific question. Must we operate in the world only with the motive to redeem our neighbors and our culture, or does common grace reset the paradigm? Gene Veith will tackle the perplexing issue of how we may learn from the world. What does common grace have to teach us about how to learn and whom we may learn from? Paul Tripp takes the issue a step further: may Christians not only live in the world but actually take pleasure in it?

Perhaps the most troubling matter of all is reconciling the idea of good unregenerate persons being condemned to hell.

How can we believe in hell or in a God who sends good people to hell? I will tackle that difficult emotional issue.

I trust that the reader will gain insight into the questions and issues raised in this introduction. Hopefully what has been puzzling, or even troubling, about the problem of good will make sense. But I also have an added agenda: to leave many readers dissatisfied with a mere introduction to the doctrine of grace. The contributing writers and I are touching on the doctrine and on the issues it speaks to. For all that is said, more is left unsaid. A comprehensive treatment of common grace will delve more extensively, for example, into the doctrine of providence. Our topics are limited to applications for individuals, but common grace has much to say about the function of the church and about its mission and relation to culture. My hope is for theologians and other writers to recognize the significance of this undertaught doctrine for strengthening the faith of Christ's followers and increasing their adoration of their Maker.

So may the reader enjoy and remain not quite satisfied, which I suppose is the case when we explore all the doctrines concerning God and his ways. He is endless joy and endless mystery. The more we delve into his mysteries, the more we are filled with awe. The more of him we take in, the more we desire to possess. What may have begun as a troubling problem to figure out becomes a doorway into more wondrous complexities—complexities that, instead of troubling us, fill us with joyful wonder.

For Discussion

1. Do you know of anyone whose faith has been tested or even abandoned because they were unable to reconcile the problem of good unregenerate people not being saved?

2. Is this problem of good the reason many young people leave the faith in college, where they find intelligent, reasonable teachers and fellow students?

3. Have you been puzzled by how some people can defy God and nevertheless produce works of beauty and even insight?

4. Have you wondered at times how good unregenerate people whom you know can be loving, compassionate, and moral?

5. Have you been troubled with the thought of how a good God could condemn them to hell?

6. Which of the following chapters intrigues you the most? Why?

PART ONE

An Exposition of the Doctrine of Common Grace

1

Restraining Sin and Wrath

Steven J. Lawson

THE DOCTRINE OF *TOTAL DEPRAVITY*, which states that unconverted people are entirely plagued by sin, begs certain questions to be asked: Why are the unrepentant not as evil as they could be? Why are those who are dead in trespasses and sins not fully immersed in a life of complete iniquity? And why is society not more perverse than it is?

These questions raise another set of questions: Why does God allow unbelievers to continue to live? Did not God say that in the day man sins, he will surely die? Yet people do not immediately die after their first sin. Why does God not strike down every transgressor the very moment they break the Law?

Admittedly these are challenging questions that deserve careful thought. More importantly, they demand biblical answers. Mere philosophical speculations will not suffice. The issue is what God himself says in his inspired Word.

The answers to these thought-provoking questions concern a theological teaching in Scripture known as the doctrine of common grace. This truth expounds the fact that God's goodness is extended to all, even to unbelievers. Though the term *common grace* is not found in the Bible, its teaching most certainly is. By way of comparison, the same could be said of the doctrine of the Trinity. Although this word is not used in

3

Scripture, this biblical truth is clearly set forth throughout its pages. So it is with common grace.

In this chapter our investigation of common grace will address God's universal kindness in restraining sin in the lives of unbelievers. Divine mercy holds back the unbelieving world from degenerating into a more corrupt depravity. By his common goodness, God refrains unregenerate people from becoming as wicked as they could possibly be. In his divine benevolence, he prevents further moral decay of the sinner and of society.

What is more, God temporarily withholds his just wrath from sinners. In so doing he chooses not to inflict immediate vengeance upon this world. Divine mercy stays the instant execution of his death sentence. Both of these spiritual realities—restraining man's sin and restraining God's wrath—will be the focus of this chapter.

God's Restraint of Sin

In Scripture there are numerous passages that teach of the divine restraint of sin in the lives of unbelievers. Such a gracious hindrance by God prevents mankind from plunging deeper into a life of iniquity. The biblical testimony of this truth will be set forth under the following ten headings, each one drawn from both the Old and New Testaments. We will approach them consecutively as they appear in the biblical record.

Sin Restrained by God's Spirit

First, sin is restrained in the lives of unbelievers by the ministry of the Holy Spirit. In the days before the flood God's Spirit held back the unregenerate from a full pursuit of wickedness. The book of Genesis states,

> When man began to multiply on the face of the land and daughters were born to them, the sons of God saw that the daughters of man were attractive. And they took as their wives

any they chose. Then the Lᴏʀᴅ said, "My Spirit shall not abide in man forever, for he is flesh: his days shall be 120 years." (Gen. 6:1–3)

This passage states that as the human race increased in number, illicit sexual acts were committed between the daughters of men and the sons of God. This likely refers to the ungodly daughters of Cain cohabitating with the godly line of Seth.[1] These grievous acts were carried out despite the resistance of the Holy Spirit. By this, God was holding them back from the full practice of their evil passions. Ultimately there came a point at which God withdrew the restraining influence of his Spirit, turning this generation over to their own sinful lusts.

So it is in this present hour. There remains the ongoing ministry of the Holy Spirit, who strives with unconverted men in order to restrain them from being as sinful as their immoral imaginations would lead them to be. This is a general restraint upon their lives, impeding them from being fully engrossed in their sins. This work of the Spirit does not necessarily bring about the regeneration of sinful men, only their restraint in sin.

Sin Restrained by Capital Punishment

Second, sin is restrained in society by the establishment of capital punishment. After the flood in the days of Noah, God sought to protect human life in the face of man's gross violence against fellow human beings. Consequently, God instituted the practice of capital punishment as a restraint against such sinful acts of aggression. "Whoever sheds the blood of man, by man shall his blood be shed, for God made man in his own image"(Gen. 9:6).

Following the flood, God established the basic principle of equitable justice that the punishment must fit the crime. If anyone deliberately takes the life of another person, the life of the evil aggressor must be taken. This presupposes that the person charged is justly tried and found guilty and that the death penalty is executed by established authorities. Such retribution was established by God to restrain evil men from committing further acts of murder. This was an act of common grace intended for the protection and preservation of human life.

The same is true today. Civil laws requiring the death penalty in the case of homicide are an extension of God's common grace. Established by the government, these laws serve to restrain the evil acts of sinful men. By this retribution all citizens are hindered in their pursuit of evil. But if these laws are removed, the restraining grace of God is likewise withdrawn.

Sin Restrained by Divine Providence

Third, sin is restrained by divine intervention in the affairs of men. In the days of Abraham, God restrained the unconverted king of Gerar, Abimelech, from the sin that he intended to do against Sarah. God hindered the king from fulfilling the lustful intentions of his depraved heart. He said to Abimelech, "It was I who kept you from sinning against me. Therefore I did not let you touch her" (Gen. 20:6).

Because God providentially prevented Abimelech from lying with Sarah, the king was kept from committing adultery. If God had not intervened, Abimelech could have also fathered a child by Sarah. Although the Bible doesn't give an explicit explanation of how God restrained the king from pursuing his lustful intention, God did restrain the sin of this unconverted man in an act of common grace.

This same preventative providence is active today as the Holy Spirit hinders evil people from committing sinful acts. This general mercy of God often holds back those controlled by lustful passions from spiraling downward into yet deeper moral filth. For example, there may be the providential cancellation of an airplane flight that prevents an individual from traveling to pursue an adulterous affair. This divine mercy may present itself through the loss of a job, which then restrains someone from having the purchasing power to participate in gross sin.

6

It may be that one's lustful intentions are discovered by another person, forcing the sin to be abandoned. Countless other scenarios can be described in which God providentially restrains evil men from the pursuit of their sin.

Sin Restrained by Limiting Satan

Fourth, sin is restrained by God's sovereign control over Satan. The Devil is a finite being, limited by divine authority. The evil one can attack individuals only to the extent that God allows. In the days of Job, God restricted Satan and the evil that he purposed to do. God and Satan had the following exchange concerning Job:

> And the LORD said to Satan, "Have you considered my servant Job, that there is none like him on the earth, a blameless and upright man, who fears God and turns away from evil?" Then Satan answered the LORD and said, "Does Job fear God for no reason? Have you not put a hedge around him and his house and all that he has, on every side? You have blessed the work of his hands, and his possessions have increased in the land. But stretch out your hand and touch all that he has, and he will curse you to your face." And the LORD said to Satan, "Behold, all that he has is in your hand. Only against him do not stretch out your hand." So Satan went out from the presence of the LORD. (Job 1:8–12)

By his own sovereign prerogative, God initiated this conversation with Satan that led to Job being tested in the furnace of affliction. With sinister design, the Devil attempted to turn Job against God. But God set the boundaries for the Devil's intended fury. The serpent of old could bring against the protagonist Job only a tribulation that was divinely limited.

To this hour, Satan continuously seeks to tempt and lure people into sin. Scripture testifies, "Your adversary the devil prowls around like a roaring lion, seeking someone to devour" (1 Peter 5:8). But the enemy is restrained by God to act only as far as God permits and no further. All the evil attacks of Satan are under the complete control of God. Though these acts are evil in themselves, God overrules them for good. What is true of believers is also true of unbelievers. By common grace Satan is restrained in his attacks against those made in God's image.

Sin Restrained by Godly Lives

Fifth, Jesus Christ taught that sin is retrained in an evil world by the preserving influence of believers. Christians are to have a powerful influence in this world, much like salt acts as a preservative agent. Speaking to his disciples, Jesus asserted, "You are the salt of the earth, but if salt has lost its taste, how shall its saltiness be restored? It is no longer good for anything except to be thrown out and trampled under people's feet" (Matt. 5:13). Jesus makes the point that his disciples are like salt in the world. Salt is a preservative that retards spoilage and withholds corruption. So it is that all followers of Christ are a preservative influence in this world, slowing down moral decay and spiritual spoilage. Their godly character acts as a purifying power that restrains the wasting away of the world.

Concerning this truth, the apostle Paul added, "Let your speech always be gracious, seasoned with salt, so that you may know how you ought to answer each person" (Col. 4:6). This is to say that a believer's speech should act as a purifying influence in the world. As Christians carry on their daily conversations, they expose sin in the world. This has a restraining effect upon unbelievers as they pursue their sinful practices. As Christ's disciples bear witness of God, they exert a moral restraint, causing evil men's participation in sin to be suppressed.

This is yet another example of common grace as God strategically places believers as restraining agents in the world. By this divine benevolence unbelievers are held back in their lustful desires for sin through the preserving influence of Christ's disciples.

Sin Restrained by Family Relationships

Sixth, Scripture indicates that sin is divinely restrained through a love that God implants within family relationships. Jesus taught this when he reasoned,

> Or which one of you, if his son asks him for bread, will give him a stone? Or if he asks for a fish, will give him a serpent? If you then, who are evil, know how to give good gifts to your children, how much more will your Father who is in heaven give good things to those who ask him! (Matt. 7:9–11)

By this our Lord affirms that even evil men possess a general love for their own family members that restrains them in pursuing sin. An evil father will not give a stone or a snake to his children. This verse implies that what restrains him from practicing more evil is the general benevolence extended to his sons and daughters. To this point it can be further added that love restrains his evil passions toward his wife and, no doubt, toward parents and other family members. This general compassion is surely implanted within men by God himself.

Such a restraining principle is clearly evidenced today. Many unconverted people are restrained in their pursuit of sin by their love for their spouses, children, and extended family members. These relationships often restrain the unregenerate from further participation in their sins. For example, an unsaved husband is sometimes prevented from plunging into adultery or drunkenness by his respect for his spouse and his desire not to shame his children. Many unsaved fathers have sought to be a good example for their children and, in so doing, have been curtailed from habitual sins.

Such family devotion is a divinely bestowed common grace that has even prompted many couples to attend church for the good of their marriages and their children. This desire for the good of loved ones has proved to be a restraining influence in many unconverted lives.

Sin Restrained by Divine Knowledge

Seventh, the apostle Paul implies that the truth about God revealed in creation acts as a restraining influence in the lives of unbelievers. But when this knowledge of God is rejected, he removes these moral restraints. Paul states,

> For his invisible attributes, namely, his eternal power and divine nature, have been clearly perceived, ever since the creation of the world, in the things that have been made. So they are without excuse. For although they knew God, they did not honor him as God or give thanks to him, but they became futile in their thinking, and their foolish hearts were darkened. . . .
>
> Therefore God gave them up in the lusts of their hearts to impurity, to the dishonoring of their bodies among themselves. . . .
>
> For this reason God gave them up to dishonorable passions. For their women exchanged natural relations for those that are contrary to nature; and the men likewise gave up natural relations with women and were consumed with passion for one another, men committing shameless acts with men and receiving in themselves the due penalty for their error.
>
> And since they did not see fit to acknowledge God, God gave them up to a debased mind to do what ought not to be done. (Rom. 1:20–21, 24, 26–28)

All creation bears unmistakable witness to the existence and attributes of God. This belief in the reality and being of God serves as a restraint to man's sin. This sense of accountability to the Creator suppresses the evil acts of man to some degree. A restraining influence is placed upon the lustful impulses of unbelievers through their inward sense of God. This general revelation about God in creation places some limitation on their pursuit of iniquity in this fallen world.

But when this divine knowledge is rejected, God sovereignly gives them over to their own degrading passions. The moral restraint that comes from the knowledge of God is removed as the sinner plunges deeper into idolatry. At some point the God-rejecter is completely abandoned by God. The result is that the sinner runs headlong into sexual perversions and unnatural affections that, in turn, lead to a depraved mind. The force that has been holding back these sins has been the knowledge of God derived from observing the created universe. This truth about God as Creator and Judge tempers the evil impulses of unsaved men.

Sin Restrained by Inner Conscience

Eighth, the apostle Paul emphatically teaches that sin is restricted by the warnings of one's conscience. Even within an unbeliever the human conscience is an effective restraint against the unhindered pursuit of sin. Paul presents the degree to which unbelievers are lost when he argues,

> For when Gentiles, who do not have the law, by nature do what the law requires, they are a law to themselves, even though they do not have the law. They show that the work of the law is written on their hearts, while their conscience also bears witness, and their conflicting thoughts accuse or even excuse them. (Rom. 2:14–15)

In other words, the human conscience serves as the inner witness that enables men and women to make a proper moral evaluation between right and wrong. The divine law is written upon every human heart. Spiritual death does not deactivate the activity of conscience. What is recorded in the Scripture regarding morality is, in a general sense, written upon the unconverted heart. Unbelievers' consciences either accuse them of wrongdoing or excuse them of right doing. They instinctively know what is wrong and feel some restraint from pursuing it. When they violate their consciences they heap upon themselves feelings of guilt, which become a restraint toward sin.

This awareness of sin, even in the hearts of unbelievers, is the common grace of God at work. The human conscience restrains unconverted men in their participation in sin by bringing about a stinging accusation of wrongdoing. Though an unbeliever may persist in sin, he will nevertheless feel some general restraint in his pursuit of it.

Sin Restrained by Human Government

Ninth, the apostle Paul also notes that sin is restrained by the divine establishment of human government. Civil authorities are put in place by God to reward good and to restrain sin in a fallen world. The apostle Paul writes,

> Let every person be subject to the governing authorities. For there is no authority except from God, and those that exist have been instituted by God. Therefore whoever resists the authorities resists what God has appointed, and those who resist will incur judgment. For rulers are not a terror to good conduct, but to bad. Would you have no fear of the one who is in authority? Then do what is good, and you will receive his approval, for he is God's servant for your good. But if you do wrong, be afraid, for he does not bear the sword in vain. For he is the servant of God, an avenger who carries out God's wrath on the wrongdoer. Therefore one must be in subjection, not only to avoid God's wrath but also for the sake of conscience. (Rom. 13:1–5)

This biblical text states that human government derives its authority from God himself. As the sovereign Ruler of the universe, God has established the institution of government over its citizens for the good of the people. The Lord has appointed government officials to punish evildoers who break the government's laws. These civil laws and their corresponding punishments act as deterrents to crime. Legal codes help to restrain evil while protecting life and property. The powers that be are to administer wrath against those who take the life of another.

The government even bears "the sword" and is, therefore, to wield it in capital punishment.

To this day, any government that establishes just laws and corresponding punishments serves as a restrainer of sin and as a preventative restriction against crimes of lawlessness. This is an extension of the common grace of God, namely his goodness in preventing further participation in evil by that government's citizens.

Sin Restrained by Gospel Truth

Tenth, the author of Hebrews indicates that unbelievers who hear the words of gospel truth are, in some tangible way, restricted in their sin. This restraint of sin is the general conviction that accompanies all gospel preaching. The author of Hebrews writes,

> For it is impossible, in the case of those who have once been enlightened, who have tasted the heavenly gift, and have shared in the Holy Spirit, and have tasted the goodness of the word of God and the powers of the age to come, and then have fallen away, to restore them again to repentance, since they are crucifying once again the Son of God to their own harm and holding him up to contempt. (Heb. 6:4–6)

These verses teach that there is a general enlightenment that the Spirit gives through the gospel. Although this illumination falls short of the special, saving work of the Spirit, this initial orientation to truth leads an unbeliever to taste the gospel but not to swallow it. Such an unconverted person becomes a mere partaker of the Spirit's ministry but not an inward possessor of it. This individual experiences the Spirit's power but does not exercise saving faith in Christ. Instead, he falls away from the very entrance into the kingdom. It is impossible to renew this person again to this place of repentance. By his unbelief, he crucifies the Lord Jesus Christ and tramples underfoot his precious blood.

Under the preaching of the gospel, unbelievers experience moral restraint as a result of hearing the truth. They are gripped by the message, though not grounded in it. These who hear the gospel receive the general blessing that accompanies hearing the truth even if they never receive saving faith. This is the moral restraint of God's common grace.

God's Restraint of Wrath

A second aspect of the doctrine of common grace is God's restraint of his immediate wrath upon sinful men. That sinners are not directly consigned to hell the moment they sin is clear evidence of his general love to them. This postponement of divine vengeance is the result of his patience and longsuffering for sinners. Let us now consider this withholding of divine judgment.

Wrath Restrained in the Garden

At the dawn of civilization, God pronounced the sentence of death upon the one who sins against him. God emphatically stated that all sin—even the first sin—must be punished by death. Yet when Adam and Eve ate from the forbidden fruit, they did not immediately die physically.

> "But of the tree of the knowledge of good and evil you shall not eat, for in the day that you eat of it you shall surely die." . . .
>
> So when the woman saw that the tree was good for food, and that it was a delight to the eyes, and that the tree was to be desired to make one wise, she took of its fruit and ate, and she also gave some to her husband who was with her, and he ate. Then the eyes of both were opened, and they knew that they were naked. And they sewed fig leaves together and made themselves loincloths. (Gen. 2:17; 3:6–7)

Death was promised to the one who breaks God's moral law. This would result in death at every level—physically, spiritually, and even eternally. But Adam and Eve chose to disobey God. Amazingly, the lives of the disobedient pair were not immediately taken. After they ate the prohibited food, they remained alive. The execution of the death penalty was delayed for years as God demonstrated his patience toward them.

The fact is, the moment that Adam and Eve sinned they died spiritually and became separated from God. Likewise, the lifelong process of physical death began, resulting in aging and eventual death. Nevertheless, their lives were not instantly required of them by God.

Since this original sin, most members of the human race have not immediately died or been subjected to hell at the moment they sinned. For the millennia since, unbelieving sinners have been allowed to live for many years, despite their initial and continued acts of sin. Though God promised death, he is longsuffering and has withheld the infliction of his immediate punishment. This temporal delay of divine vengeance is an expression of his common grace toward both nonelect and elect sinners. God lovingly postpones his eternal condemnation in order to extend time for unbelievers to repent. By this, God gives prolonged opportunities for even the reprobate to come to saving faith in Christ.

Wrath Restrained before the Flood

Further, divine wrath was restrained in the days before the flood. Persistent unbelief in God and rampant sexual immorality demanded his immediate judgment, but he nevertheless remained patient toward sinners. The biblical account reads, "Then the LORD said, 'My Spirit shall not abide in man forever, for he is flesh: his days shall be 120 years'" (Gen. 6:3).

Throughout the one hundred twenty years during which Noah built the ark, God delayed the wrath that justly deserved to be unleashed upon the entire human race. During this prolonged period, divine vengeance was restrained against guilty sinners, giving them extended time to repent. In the days of

Noah, this longsuffering of God (1 Peter 3:20) was his common grace toward mankind.

In every subsequent era of human history God has, likewise, been longsuffering toward unrepentant sinners though they have continued to engross themselves in their pursuit of iniquity. To this present hour God remains forbearing toward those who flaunt his moral law and live in flagrant sin. Despite the mounting iniquities of this adulterous generation God gives repeated opportunities to the unbelieving world to turn from their sins and believe in his Son, Jesus Christ.

Wrath Restrained during the Incarnation

Even when God chose to bring his immediate wrath upon sinners, he chose to do so not with the majority but with the minority. Luke's gospel gives account of God's immediate judgment upon isolated individuals during Christ's earthly ministry, though he postponed punishing the many. Luke records,

> There were some present at that very time who told him about the Galileans whose blood Pilate had mingled with their sacrifices. And he answered them, "Do you think that these Galileans were worse sinners than all the other Galileans, because they suffered in this way? No, I tell you; but unless you repent, you will all likewise perish. Or those eighteen on whom the tower in Siloam fell and killed them: do you think that they were worse offenders than all the others who lived in Jerusalem? No, I tell you; but unless you repent, you will all likewise perish." (Luke 13:1–5)

In this account Jesus responds to the sudden judgment of God upon the Galileans and those on whom the tower in Siloam fell. Both these instances involved the unexpected taking of the lives of humans who were sinful and deserved death. In response, Jesus addressed those who survived and announced that they were equally deserving of such destruction. Instead it was the longsuffering of God that had suspended divine judgment upon

16

them. By implication it was the common grace of God that withheld his swift recompense. God graciously chose to give Jesus' listeners the opportunity to repent, lest they likewise perish.

The same is true with God's wrath in this present day. Though many have denied his existence and cursed his name, God has patiently allowed these blasphemers to live a full and long life. This world is filled with God-haters and atheists who have shaken their angry fists in the face of God. Yet God has chosen to restrain his just vengeance from immediately consuming them in order to graciously grant them time to respond to him in repentance and faith.

Wrath Restrained toward the Gentiles

Moreover, the apostle Paul announced that God has restrained his wrath toward all the nations of the world. He has postponed his judgment and given them repeated opportunities to repent. Speaking at Lystra, the apostle proclaims, "In past generations he allowed all the nations to walk in their own ways" (Acts 14:16).

Paul is stating that God permitted the nations to pursue their own path. Throughout the ages, God allowed all peoples to go astray. During the long centuries he permitted them to choose their own way of life and to live in sin. In so doing God did not immediately serve the execution of the death penalty upon them, but he endured their defiance with longsuffering.

In his Areopagus address Paul proclaimed this same truth to the Athenian philosophers: "The times of ignorance God overlooked, but now he commands all people everywhere to repent" (Acts 17:30).

When Paul states that God "overlooked" their sinful ignorance, he means that God chose not to judge the pagan nations immediately for their sins. For centuries God has demonstrated patience toward unconverted man's sin and ignorance. In his common grace he temporarily stayed the sentence of death. This does not mean that God pardoned the nations of their sins. Rather, God held them accountable to him and condemned their sin, but did not immediately punish them. Their times of ignorance have now come to an end through the preaching of the gospel. Yet God remains longsuffering in withholding his immediate wrath.

Wrath Restrained toward the Jews

Similarly, the apostle Paul teaches that God has been restrained in his wrath toward the unbelieving Jewish nation. For centuries past, Israel disobeyed God, yet he momentarily withheld his death sentence upon them. Describing the spiritual state of the Jewish people, Paul explains,

> Or do you presume on the riches of his kindness and forbearance and patience, not knowing that God's kindness is meant to lead you to repentance? But because of your hard and impenitent heart you are storing up wrath for yourself on the day of wrath when God's righteous judgment will be revealed. (Rom. 2:4–5)

Throughout their history God bestowed unprecedented goodness upon his chosen people. In his kindness God gave them great material and spiritual blessings. He graced them with a bountiful land, a righteous law, a magnificent temple, a spiritual priesthood, providential care, and countless more blessings. But Israel sinned repeatedly against him. In response God patiently endured their many transgressions and rebellions. Even when Israel crucified God's Son he patiently endured, with much longsuffering, this rebellious nation.

God's delaying of his judgment does not deny its inescapable reality; that day of final reckoning is coming soon. The unbelieving nation is storing up wrath until it will be unleashed on the final day. In the end God's righteous judgment will be executed in all its fury. However, common grace is presently holding back God's wrath and providing an extended time for the Jewish people to repent.

Wrath Restrained toward the Unbelieving

Finally, the apostle Peter teaches that God temporarily stays his judgment toward the unbeliever, giving them further opportunity to repent. In his second epistle Peter states: "The Lord is not slow to fulfill his promise as some count slowness, but is patient toward you, not wishing that any should perish, but that all should reach repentance" (2 Peter 3:9). According to this text God delays the return of Christ because of his grace and mercy toward sinners. In so doing he allows them additional opportunity to turn from their sins and believe in Christ. At the appointed time, when the last of the elect has trusted in him, Jesus will return. But this present delay is a gracious period of postponed judgment that is pending for the unregenerate.

Though some believers do not understand why God chooses to withhold his judgment, the reason lies in his patience toward the unbelieving. While it is the general desire of God that all men be saved, he has not decreed the redemption of all. In the face of the world's unbelief he graciously provides extended time for sinners to repent. It is his common grace that gives this expanded opportunity to impenitent sinners.

By His Grace, for His Glory

Every blessing, whether physical or spiritual, that comes into the lives of sinful human beings is the direct result of God's grace. Saving grace is unto the glory of God (Eph. 1:6, 12, 14), but so also is common grace to the praise of his glory. Ultimately, the truth of God's universal benevolence to all mankind should lead every believer to praise his holy name.

This was the invitation of the psalmist as he called upon every believer to give praise to the Lord for his goodness to all. The psalmist David declares,

The LORD is good to all,
>   and his mercy is over all that he has made.

All your works shall give thanks to you, O LORD,
>   and all your saints shall bless you! (Ps. 145:9–10)

With common grace clearly in mind, David urges all believers to consider God's goodness to all and his mercies over all his works. As we meditate upon God's kindness to all—including his restraint of sin and his withholding of immediate judgment upon this depraved world—our response must be to rise up and bless the Lord.

It is incumbent upon every believer to have a comprehensive knowledge of God's operation of grace in this world. In so doing, we as believers must extol and magnify the Lord for his common grace in much the same way as we praise him for his saving grace. As you contemplate the common grace of God, just as the psalmist David did, does this glorious truth stir up the same response within your own heart?

For Discussion

1. Are you familiar with the doctrine of total depravity? The Westminster Confession of Faith explains it as coming from the corruption of our original parents, "whereby we are utterly indisposed, disabled, and made opposite to all good, and wholly inclined to all evil" (WCF 6.4). Would you agree with this doctrine?

2. How does common grace explain why total depravity does not result in totally depraved behavior?

3 The author gives ten ways in which God restrains sin. Can you give examples of any of the ways listed that you have observed or even experienced in your own life?

4. For what purposes would God restrain sin? Think in terms of his own character and his purposes for man.

5. Do you ever question the justice of God? Do the answers that the author gives help you to understand what seems like undue delay or even misapplied justice?

6. How should understanding God's purposes for restraining his wrath affect how you exercise restraint of your own anger, even righteous anger?

7. Does God's restraint lead you to worship him for his "universal benevolence to all mankind"?

2

My Father's World: The Good Gifts of Common Grace

Sean Michael Lucas

LATE AFTERNOON on Sunday, February 10, 2013, my town, Hattiesburg, Mississippi, was hit by an EF-4 tornado. As the tornado moved from the western part of our area through the business and shopping district to the University of Southern Mississippi and its neighborhoods, the Lord graciously allowed the storm to skip through town rather than to remain on the ground the entire time. Though it went more than fifteen miles through our area and was three-quarters of a mile wide, the tornado's devastation was far less than it could have been.

In the aftermath, as people assessed the damage, cleaned up, and helped to rebuild, a range of questions—theological ones at that—came to mind. Why did the Lord allow the tornado to hit one house but not the one directly beside it? Why did the Lord direct the storm so that it hit one Presbyterian church in midtown, but not our Presbyterian church on the west side (though the tornado passed directly in front of our building)? More particularly, why did so many of our church members lose their homes or experience significant damage, but unbelievers and scoffers against God and faith were not affected at all?

23

Other questions came to me during the cleanup. Not only did teams come from various Presbyterian Church in America congregations and presbyteries as well as from other Protestant denominations, but also groups of people—believers and unbelievers alike—went to clean up and rebuild areas that they would not have willingly visited otherwise. What accounts for that sort of neighborliness? Why did unbelievers want their neighbors to be restored and their places to be made whole? Why was our city largely preserved from looting as unbelievers as well as believers loved their neighbors well?

The answers to many of these questions are found in the biblical teaching that we call common grace. We typically think about common grace as moving in two directions. One direction is *restraint*—the restraint of the effects of sin in our world and in human relationship. The other direction is *bestowal*—the bestowal of good gifts from God on our world and in and through human relationships. Theologian John Murray put it this way: "Common grace is more than negative and preventative; it is also positive, in the bestowal and protection of good. God not only restrains the destructive effects of sin in nature but he also causes nature to teem with the gifts of his goodness."[1] Thus, when we think about the "bestowal" side of God's common grace, we are thinking about God's determination to care for his good world by continuing to provide good gifts to and through human beings for the purposes of human repentance and redemption as well as divine glory.

God's Good World

The reason why nature continues to teem with good gifts is because this world belongs to God as the Creator. "The earth is the LORD's and the fullness thereof," Psalm 24:1 tells us, "the world and those who dwell therein." God did not create the world and then set it loose. He certainly did not cede control of his world to Satan, though the enemy has invaded and attempted to usurp God's world (Eph. 2:2; 6:12). Rather, this world continues to be our Father's world, which he entrusted to human beings as stewards in the garden of Eden—a trust that he has not revoked, limited, or amended.

The world that God the Creator made bubbled forth with goodness and potential (cf. Ps. 19:1). In Genesis 1–2, the picture emerges that this world is good, fit for human beings, full of life and light. God speaks and the sun and moon emerge; God speaks and waters separate, skies form, seas fill; God speaks and the earth sprouts vegetation and plants and fruit trees; God speaks and the waters fill with all sorts of fishes and living creatures; God speaks and the earth brings forth animals and livestock and creeping things. This was a world that was teeming with life, displaying God's goodness.

And the garden of Eden was especially fitted for human life. "The Lord God planted a garden in Eden, in the east. . . . And out of the ground the Lord God made to spring up every tree that is pleasant to the sight and good for food. The tree of life was in the midst of the garden, and the tree of the knowledge of good and evil" (Gen. 2:8–9). This was no scanty provision that God provided, but rather a world filled with possibility and life. As Calvin noted, "[God] has so wonderfully adorned heaven and earth with as unlimited abundance, variety, and beauty of all things as could possibly be, quite like a spacious and splendid house, provided and filled with the most exquisite and at the same time most abundant furnishings."[2] This was God's good world.

When God made human beings, they shared in the goodness of that world. God actually formed Adam from the stuff of earth as well as the stuff of heaven (Gen. 2:7), signaling Adam's solidarity with the rest of creation while also distinguishing him from it. That distinction from creation was founded in the fact that Adam was created in the image of God (Gen. 1:26–27). Because all human beings share their descent from Adam, they share his solidarity with creation and the commonality of being made in God's image.

Likewise there was a common mandate, one that all humans share in Adam: "Be fruitful and multiply and fill the earth and subdue it and have dominion over the fish of the sea and over the birds of the heavens and over every living thing that moves on the earth" (Gen. 1:28). This common mandate to be fruitful, to multiply and fill, to subdue and have dominion over God's world would be fulfilled in a variety of ways. It would require applying human creativity and intelligence to God's world to bring out its full potential and flourishing—how else would the world be filled? And it would require establishing and managing structures in order to bring the world to order and subjection—how else would Adam and his posterity rule it? As human beings lived out this mandate, they would truly glorify and enjoy God and his goodness, wisdom, and power—because they would be living in God's good world, provided for them as a father graciously takes care to do whatever is necessary for his own beloved children.

And yet, even as humankind shares in this solidarity, there is also diversity. In the same way that the trees produce after their own kind and the animals produce after their kind—suggesting the importance of diversity in God's world—"God created man in his own image, in the image of God he created him; male and female he created them" (Gen. 1:27). The fact that God created man and woman to share common humanity as well as diverse gifts and functions within that humanity, and that they image forth humankind together, suggests the continued significance of diversity in showing forth the glorious potential of God's good world. The difference in gifts—not just between Adam and Eve, but between all humans—was necessary in order to show forth God's image; all of humanity collectively in their diversity and solidarity display God's image.

And God embedded certain laws to guide the development of this good world he had made. In the same way that the vegetation and animals would reproduce after their own kind, human civilization and culture would operate in the light of these laws or norms. These creational laws, which were part of the very fabric of creation, served as standards for the right and wrong way of doing things. They were summed up in the law regarding the tree of the knowledge of good and evil, but they also guided naming the animals, marrying and child-bearing, and tending and guarding the garden. As humans operated within those norms, they would bring creation to its proper flourishing in line with God's word and purpose.[3]

While Adam's rebellion disrupted God's original intention for his creation and creatures, it did not destroy that intention. It is notable that God still expects Adam to work the ground, though it would now work against him (Gen. 3:17–19); and it is notable that God gives Noah the same command that he had given Adam, that Noah and his sons would be fruitful and multiply and fill the earth (Gen. 9:1). Moreover, after the fall, human beings demonstrate their obedience to God's mandate—they fill the earth with human beings; they tend the earth and the flocks; they build cities, make music, and forge items of bronze and iron (Gen. 4:17–22). And even though Adam disobeyed God's fundamental creational norm, still that norm continues to operate—the practical wisdom for living life in God's world shows itself in remarkable creativity and human flourishing.

To be sure, this creative activity bears the marks of human sinfulness: Lamech sings a song of vengeance to his wives (Gen. 4:23–24); Noah cultivates a vineyard after he leaves the ark, gets drunk, and exposes himself to be shamed by his son (Gen. 9:20–23); the peoples of the earth attempt to build a tower to heaven, evidence that "nothing that they propose to do will now be impossible for them" (Gen. 11:1–6). And yet creative activity in God's world was not condemned; it was part of the mandate to fill, subdue, and have dominion over God's world, which continues to this day (Ps. 8:5–8).

Because human beings continue to bear God's image and to live out God's mandate as they work in God's world, all this activity serves as revelation of God. Of course it is marred by human sinfulness; yet humans can still see God's goodness, power, and wisdom revealed in his creation, his creatures, and their creativity. This revelation is what theologians call "general revelation," and it continues in this world by "common grace." And God calls us to meditate on this revelation and grace so that we might be drawn to him. "There is no doubt," Calvin wrote,

> that the Lord would have us uninterruptedly occupied in this holy meditation; that, while we contemplate in all creatures, as in mirrors, those immense riches of his wisdom, justice, goodness, and power, we should not merely run over them curiously, and, so to speak, with a fleeting glance; but we should ponder them at length, turn them over in our minds seriously and faithfully, and recollect them repeatedly. [4]

Indeed, humans should see God's power and godhead, his goodness and wisdom, in the flourishing of God's good world and they should trust in him (Rom. 1:19–20).

God's Good Care

God, however, did not create the world and leave it to humans' care or destruction. Rather, he continues to care well for his own world in ways that we would attribute to common grace. God cares for the birds of the air, feeding them, and for the lilies of the field, clothing them (Matt. 6:26–30). In fact, God provides food for all his creatures: "He gives to the beasts their food, and to the young ravens that cry" (Ps. 147:9). And if God provides this way for creatures not made in his image, he surely provides for human beings, whether they obey him or not. As Paul noted, "[God] did not leave himself without witness, for he did good by giving you rains from heaven and fruitful seasons, satisfying your hearts with food and gladness" (Acts 14:17). He provided food and drink, rain from heaven, good work to do, marriage and children, joy and gladness—regardless of whether humans obeyed him or not (Eccl. 5:18–20;

Matt. 5:44–45; Luke 6:35–36; 16:25). Unbelievers as well as believers know prosperity and health, blessing and peace in this life (Ps. 73:3–5; Matt. 19:16–24; Luke 12:13–21). These "good things" are part of God's continued, beneficent care.

Often God uses believers to bless unbelievers and thus serve as instruments of his continued kindness and care toward them. From the time of the promise to Abraham, those who trust God and follow him were to be a blessing to all the families of the earth (Gen. 12:1–3). So God sends Jacob to Laban in order to bless him financially (Gen. 30:27); he sends Joseph to Egypt to preserve not only Israel's life but the lives of Egyptian unbelievers as well (Gen. 39:5; 45:5); and even in the exile, God sends Israel to Babylon, not only for Israel's punishment but also for Babylon's blessing (Jer. 29:7). Perhaps the greatest example of this is Daniel: he stands as God's representative of blessing to Nebuchadnezzar and Darius. In all these examples we see God's determination to show kindness to pagans through his own people—and this is common grace.

In addition, God exercises his good care of the world through unbelievers themselves. That is to say, unbelievers do "good" things even if they do them with selfish motives or sinful purposes. For example, unbelievers know loving affections and do loving actions, a kind of neighborliness: "If you love those who love you," Jesus observed, "what reward do you have? Do not even tax collectors do the same? And if you greet only your brothers, what more are you doing than others? Do not even the Gentiles do the same?" (Matt. 5:46–47). Private, self-interested love is still viewed as a good gift even when practiced by unbelievers. This kind of love serves to foster and preserve human relationships and society.

And of course the best example of this kind of love, natural affection, and neighborliness in unbelievers is the relationship between parents and children. Unbelievers have a natural affection for their children; in fact, one of the marks of extreme depravity is the loss of such affection (Rom. 1:30; 2 Tim. 3:2).

As unbelievers show love to their children, though their love is naturally private, self-interested, and less than truly virtuous, they show forth that they have received one of the good gifts of God through which God cares for his world.

Not only do unbelievers love one another, but they also have a conscience that serves to ground justice and fair dealing in this world—and this is a God-given gift that preserves God's world (Rom. 2:14–15). Because human beings are typically able to agree upon general principles of equity, society is sustained and even flourishes—laws are developed and enforced, market exchange is regulated, property is respected. Government is possible, indeed is actual, because of this God-given gift of conscience. Magistrates rise up in given cultures to punish evil and to reward good (1 Peter 2:14), and these rulers are given, instituted, and appointed by God "for your good" (see Rom. 13:1–4). While governments certainly may become corrupt, that does not negate the fact that, when they function remotely well, they provide an approximation of peace, justice, and goodness (1 Tim. 2:1–2). Surely this is a divine gift, a common grace, to preserve God's creation and creatures.

Moreover, unbelievers and believers alike are able to explore God's creation and so bring it to a measure of flourishing, despite the curse upon the ground that increases the difficulty of our labors. The arts—not just fine art, but popular art and folk art along with music and dance—mirror God's creative action by creatively exploring God's world. After all, God's world continues to display God's power, goodness, and wisdom, and human beings were made to reflect upon and reflect back that divine glory in mimicking God's creation (Rom. 1:20). When art mirrors back God's beauty in his world, whether knowingly or unknowingly, it does this only by means of God's general grace to humankind. And both believers and unbelievers can produce such arts; they are part of the "natural gifts" of God to his creatures.[5]

Science is also a divine gift that God continues to use to care for his world through humans. The nineteenth-century theologian Abraham Kuyper insisted that science was part of God's original creation purposes: "Science belongs to *the creation*. Just think: if our human life had developed in its paradise situation, apart from sin, then science would have existed there just as it exists now, even though its development would obviously have been entirely different."[6] And that is because science serves as a means of human exploration of God's world—medicine is the exploration of the human body; mathematics is the exploration of God's orderly world; engineering and architecture are the application of human intellect to natural resources to create new structures, processes, and technology. These activities are not merely human or secular, but are given to humans by divine grant.

Furthermore, another good gift that God gives to humans is the ability to produce literature of different kinds. Whether it is philosophical writing from the ancient philosophers, whether it is historical narrative that speaks of the wars of kings and princes, whether it is sociological analysis that describes human beings in this world, whether it is poetry and wisdom literature that sings of human love and human relationships, whether it is fiction that reflects something of wisdom, goodness, and justice—all these kinds of writing are God's gift to human beings. "Shall we count anything praiseworthy or noble without recognizing at the same time that it comes from God?" Calvin held. "Those men whom Scripture calls 'natural men' were, indeed, sharp and penetrating in their investigation of inferior things. Let us, accordingly, learn by their example how many gifts the Lord left to human nature even after it was despoiled of its true good."[7]

Indeed, we view the arts, science, and literature as good divine gifts because God is the source of all truth in his world. Not only does God's creation continue to reveal him and his truth through these gifts, but God himself continues to work in and through humans to make this the case. "If we regard the Spirit of God as the sole fountain of truth, we shall neither reject the truth itself, nor despise it wherever it shall appear, unless we wish to dishonor the Spirit of God. For by holding the gifts of the Spirit in slight esteem, we contemn and reproach the Spirit himself," Calvin argued. Whatever is praiseworthy in areas of human endeavor and brings about human flourishing actually comes about because God the Spirit is at work—even through unbelievers. Calvin continued by observing that "it is no wonder, then, that the knowledge of all that is most excellent in human life is said to be communicated to us through the Spirit of God."[8]

And so the general operations of the Spirit include working not only through those who appear to be Christians, but also through those ultimately lost souls who prophesy in Jesus' name, do good works in his name, and taste the Spirit's power (Matt. 7:21–23; Heb. 6:4–6). According to Calvin, we can see God's Spirit at work generally anytime human beings, whether converted or not, flourish in ways that show forth God's goodness, wisdom, and power. Human flourishing—even after the fall and the curse, the flood and the endless reality of decay, destruction, and death—is the result of God's continued care for his world. Through his providential provision, his people, and the Spirit's working through unbelievers, this world still evidences that it belongs to God and that he is determined to bless his creatures in and through it. Our God continues to shine through all that is fair because he is the one working his good in his world.

God's Good Purpose

God continues to care for his world through his common grace for a reason. His kindness serves as a motivation for our repentance: "Do you presume on the riches of his kindness and forbearance and patience, not knowing that God's kindness is meant to lead you to repentance?" (Rom. 2:4). Even though human beings rebel against him, God continues to give good gifts to his world as a means to woo and win them back to repentance. As unbelievers are confronted with their ingratitude, space is opened in their hearts to turn to God in repentant faith.

Repentance is furthered when we recognize that we can point to nothing as humans that is our own good. Even when unbelievers bring about human flourishing they do so on the unstable foundation of self-interest at best and rebellion against God at worst. And even believers experience the reality of remaining sin in this life; any good that they do is "not at all of themselves, but wholly from the Spirit of Christ."[9] Thus, whether it comes from a believer or an unbeliever, the good that we find in our world is the result of the common operations of God's Spirit in and through the individual. Truly there is nothing good that we have not received from God's own hand (1 Cor. 4:7).

Even further, whatever good we do receive from God's hand we willfully misuse, ascribing these gifts to our own power and ability and suppressing the truth they teach us in unrighteousness (Rom. 1:18–21). These good gifts should show us the God who is there, as well as his goodness and kindness, and they should inculcate trust in him. Instead, as a result of the fall, humans inevitably abuse these gifts so that all our virtues and all our gifts are sullied before God and we lose all favor. Humans in turn worship themselves or other creatures rather than the Creator. Hence God's good gifts will serve as a judgment against humans; because humans misuse what God meant to lead them to him they stand condemned, without excuse before him (Rom. 1:20).[10]

Yet God continues to do good to human beings in order to turn their hearts back to him through repentance. For those who do receive God's effectual, special, redemptive grace, they could say that they were led to trust God in part because of his kindness in common grace. To put it succinctly, common grace is the preparation for and serves the purpose of special, redemptive grace. As John Murray noted,

> Common grace then receives at least one explanation from the fact of special grace, and special grace has its precondition and sphere of operation in common grace. Without common grace special grace would not be possible because special grace would have no material out of which to erect its structure. It is common grace that provides not only the sphere in which, but also the material out of which, the building fitly framed together may grow up into a holy temple of God.[11]

What Murray is saying is important: God's creation serves the purpose of redemption, his providential dealings with his creation find their purpose in his providential dealings with the elect, his common grace will come to fruition in redemptive grace, his world will come to full and final flourishing in the new heavens and new earth.

In other words, common grace is not redemptive in itself, yet nothing that God the Spirit does in his general grace through humanity and the creation will be lost; it will be brought into the world made new. And that is because God's purpose in redemption is nothing less than to undo the effects of the fall and to bring all creation to its intended flourishing. Paul spelled out this cosmic redemptive intention in Ephesians 1.

> In him we have redemption through his blood, the forgiveness of our trespasses, according to the riches of his grace, which he lavished upon us, in all wisdom and insight making known to us the mystery of his will, according to his purpose, which he set forth in Christ as a plan for the fullness of time, to unite all things in him, things in heaven and things on earth. (Eph. 1:7–10)

All things in heaven and on earth will be summed up, united together, tied up in Christ. In the same way that redemption deals with the wrath and the curse of God that hang over us personally and individually, so it will deal with the curse and decay that hang over God's creation—God's redemptive grace will extend to all things, whether on earth or in heaven (cf. Rom. 8:21).

Therefore, all that was good about God's creation will be brought into this new world, cleansed by the blood of Christ (Col. 1:19–20). In the heavenly Jerusalem, "the kings of the earth will bring their glory into it. . . . They will bring into it the glory and the honor of the nations" (Rev. 21:24, 26). The riches and flourishing of the nations—developed through God's common grace, cleansed by Christ's blood and judgment fires—are carried into the New Jerusalem and laid at the foot of the throne. In Isaiah's vision of the end, "the glory of Lebanon" will come into the city, "the cypress, the plane, and the pine" (Isa. 60:13); bronze and iron, silver and gold shall be in abundance; the "ships of Tarshish" (v. 9) will bring not only God's children but the riches of the nations. The goodness of God's world will not be lost but will be perfected in the new heavens and new earth.[12]

In that last day God's ultimate purpose for his general, common grace will be realized—his glory. All that was good in this world and in this age, brought about by the direction and power of God the Holy Spirit, will redound to God's honor and praise throughout all eternity. All creation—every creature that remains in the new earth, all who have washed their robes in the Lamb's blood—will see the multifaceted glory of God in the way he cared for his world and for those who dwell therein. We will see that this was and is our Father's world. He did not and would not lose it, but preserved it and brought it to full flourishing as we return to a garden that is better than Eden—the river of life, the tree of life, and the throne of God (Rev. 22:1–5). And our Father's blood-bought people will turn and see that it is all very good.

For Discussion

1. What is the connection the author makes between nature teeming with good gifts and God being the Creator?

2. For what purposes does God bestow common grace gifts to people, both regenerate and unregenerate?

3. Though common grace is not saving grace, have you seen common grace blessings lead an unbeliever to consider the gospel? Did common grace impact your own conversion?

4. What is the connection between good gifts being displayed in the unregenerate and the work of the Holy Spirit?

5. According to Calvin, what sin are we in danger of committing by not acknowledging the good contributions of the unregenerate? Does this understanding make a difference for you in being able to acknowledge good work and even goodness in the unregenerate?

6. Do you agree with the author that redemption not only applies to individual salvation but will deal with the curse and decay of the created world?

7. How does such an understanding of redemption tie in with common grace?

PART TWO

Application of Common Grace for Worship and Life

Worshiping and Glorifying the Creator and Provider

D. Marion Clark

For the beauty of the earth,
for the glory of the skies,
for the love which from our birth
over and around us lies,
Lord of all, to thee we raise
this our hymn of grateful praise.

For the beauty of each hour
of the day and of the night,
hill and vale, and tree and flow'r,
sun and moon and stars of light,
Lord of all, to thee we raise
this our hymn of grateful praise.

For the joy of ear and eye,
for the heart and mind's delight,
for the mystic harmony
linking sense to sound and sight,
Lord of all, to thee we raise
this our hymn of grateful praise.

For the joy of human love,
brother, sister, parent, child,

friends on earth, and friends above,
for all gentle thoughts and mild,
Lord of all, to thee we raise
this our hymn of grateful praise.

For each perfect gift of thine
to our race so freely giv'n,
graces human and divine,
flow'rs of earth and buds of heav'n,
Lord of all, to thee we raise
this our hymn of grateful praise.[1]

This beloved hymn, "For the Beauty of the Earth," celebrates God for his common grace gifts of creation's beauty and human love. Stanza one presents these two themes. Stanzas two and three expound upon creation's beauty. There is the beauty we see around us on earth, in nature, and beyond to the heavenly bodies of sun, moon, and stars. There is the beauty we hear, also emanating from nature. Stanza four celebrates the "joy of human love," from that of family relations to that of friendship. As the hymnist concludes in stanza five, these gifts are "to our [human] race so freely given."

This is the common grace worship of God as Creator and Provider. It is a recognition that "every good gift and every perfect gift is from above" (James 1:17). In chapter 2, Sean Lucas presented the manifold common grace gifts of God. Paul Tripp discusses in chapter 8 how and why we ought to delight in those gifts. In this chapter we are considering how they are to lead us to glorify God in our worship.

Giving Thanks and Praise to Creator and Provider

Simply put, we are to thank and praise him! "All your works shall give thanks to you, O LORD" (Ps. 145:10). We are works of our Creator, and we are to join with the rest of creation in giving thanks for God's workmanship. We are to thank him that he deigned to create us and the rest of creation. He did not need to do so. We are to thank him not only that he created us all but also that we are wondrously made. "I praise you, for I am fearfully and wonderfully made. Wonderful are your works; my soul knows it very well" (Ps. 139:14). The human body and life is a wondrous work, and so are all God's works. If "the heavens declare the glory of God, and the sky above proclaims his handiwork" (Ps. 19:1), then we too are to glorify our Maker, giving thanks and praise to him for everything that he has made and that he continues to provide.

We need to worship by counting our blessings; we need to name them one by one. Such an action helps us to lift the burdens that come our way, but more to the point is that it leads us to give God his rightful due. Have you thanked God for his common grace gifts to you today? There are more than you probably recognized. As I write this in the spring, I look out the window and am thankful to God that he granted a clear sky and warm sunshine. The trees are sprouting their new leaves. These gifts are easy to see and yet all the more easy to ignore for most of the day. This year's spring has been colder than usual, with many overcast days. I grumble about the cold without thanking God for my warm bed and home, or for my coat to keep me warm as I walk to church—which I can do because God has kept me healthy. There simply is not an instance in which blessings are not all around me, if only I would take notice, and then while taking notice give thanks to God. Perhaps this is what the apostle Paul had in mind when he instructed us, "in everything by prayer and supplication with thanksgiving let your request be made known to God" (Phil. 4:6).

When we are burdened with a load of care, we should "take it to the Lord in prayer."[2] But then we should be thankful to God that he, by his common grace, takes an interest in our everyday affairs. Our Father, who delights us with robing the flowers of the field, meets our daily needs and all the more as we take an interest in seeking his kingdom. He is not so caught up in the big picture that he forgets to provide the "little" gifts, if we would but take notice of them and give thanks to him.

But these are not such little gifts, and they are more numerous than we realize. I used to have the mind-set that we can always be thankful for our salvation, even when we have nothing else. But we never have "nothing else." We have past, present, and future gifts from our Creator and Provider. We are fed, we are clothed, and we have human relationships. Our problem is not what we lack but what we fail to see. At this moment, you read these words because your Creator has granted you eyesight. If you are wearing glasses it is because he has provided people with skill to examine your eyes and to create eyeglasses. He has provided the means for you to purchase the glasses. Developing thankful hearts for God's common grace gifts will sharpen our ability to observe and to appreciate his gifts everywhere.

Yes, we are to be thankful to God with grateful hearts. Lack of thankfulness is what leads to a downward spiral, as Romans 1:18–32 explains. "For although they knew God, they did not honor him as God or give thanks to him, but they became futile in their thinking, and their foolish hearts were darkened" (v. 21). From there the spiral begins. God wants our thanks for everything that he gives. He wants to be acknowledged as Creator and Giver of all good things. He wants to be thanked for causing all things to work for the good of those who love him (see Rom. 8:28). It is thankfulness that glorifies him.

Thankfulness preserves the right spirit of humility as we acknowledge that nothing we possess comes from ourselves but from God. According to the Romans passage, refusing to thank God leads to pride even if we transfer our gratitude to an idol (v. 23). The idol itself is the only creation that we can attribute to our own resources—a figment of our imagination made up to serve our ego. Thankfulness and praise are necessary to keep our hearts calibrated for proper worship and service to the only God, the only Giver of all good things.

Have you ever devoted a prayer to thanking God for his gifts—a prayer in which you do nothing but thank God? Think about it. Do you not also add a petition or two? Perhaps you ask for God to make you more mindful of his bounty; very likely you ask forgiveness for not being thankful enough. Should we ask to be made more mindful and confess our sins? Of course, but beware of always concluding prayers with the focus on you. You start off thanking and praising God but end with a word about yourself. Surely God is pleased with prayer that does nothing but give him glory and thanksgiving. Surely he is pleased with prayers that give thanks for a blessing we noticed.

Thanksgiving leads to worship—ascribing to God his worthiness. As we observe the wonders of his creation, as we explore the mysteries of his providential care, as we are then led into thankfulness for these wonders and mysteries, we are moved to worship this awesome Creator. In heaven's throne room, worship is described as follows:

> And whenever the living creatures give glory and honor and thanks to him who is seated on the throne, who lives forever and ever, the twenty-four elders fall down before him who is seated on the throne and worship him who lives forever and ever. They cast their crowns before the throne, saying,

> "Worthy are you, our Lord and God,
>   to receive glory and honor and power,
> for you created all things,
>   and by your will they existed and were created."
>   (Rev. 4:9–11)

The worship of heaven involves the worship of God as Creator. We should be joining with this theme in our earthly worship. Our days should be marked with thankfulness and praise as we move throughout our waking hours. Think what a day would mean if you filled it with "thank-you's" to your Creator and Provider for his common grace blessings.

Why do we tend to show apathy instead of thanksgiving for the common grace blessings that God gives to us? The trials of life and the busyness of life certainly distract us from praising God. But there is another factor unique to the children of God. It can be difficult to be attentive to common grace blessings when we are overwhelmed with the blessing of special grace—our redemption in Jesus Christ. Redemptive grace does raise us to great heights of thanksgiving and praise. As much as we may enjoy and be thankful for standing on a mountaintop, it does not compare with the mountaintop experience of salvation through Christ. And as much as we may delight in earth's beauty and in human relations, such delights lead us to the hope of even greater beauty and love to come at the resurrection. No earthly Jerusalem compares with what we long for in the heavenly Jerusalem that is our inheritance in Christ Jesus.

And yet God's good gifts exist now. His blessings are present now. Just as a young person may be blind to what he possesses now because he is working hard for what he hopes to gain in the future, so we can be blind to the good that our heavenly Father is bestowing on us at this point in time. Even worse, we miss the opportunity to thank him and to ascribe to him the glory that is his due for "lesser" blessings.

But the common (only in the sense of being common to regenerate and unregenerate alike) grace blessings are worthy of our highest thanksgiving and praise for two reasons. First, God is worthy of thanksgiving and praise for *all* his works, because all his works are wonderful. We do not reserve our best worship effort for redemption, only to add a "by the way, thanks for the other stuff" spirit to the gifts from common grace.

If we give our attention to the gifts derived from creation, we will rise all the more to new heights of appreciation and wonder for God's goodness to us. We rightly look to the cross and ask wondrously, "Who am I that God would do such a mighty work?" But we ought to be led to such adoration by what is observable to everyone—namely, God's creation. In Psalm 8 David is led to ask wonderingly of his Creator,

> When I look at your heavens, the work of your fingers,
>   the moon and the stars, which you have set in place,
> what is man that you are mindful of him,
>   and the son of man that you care for him? (vv. 3–4)

To impress upon Job how far he is above man, God turns to his works of creation and providential care.

> Where were you when I laid the foundation of the earth?
> . . . .
>
> Have you commanded the morning since your days began,
>   and caused the dawn to know its place?
> . . . .
>
> Can you hunt the prey for the lion,
>   or satisfy the appetite of the young lions?
> . . . .
>
> Is it by your understanding that the hawk soars
>   and spreads his wings toward the south?
>   (Job 38:4,12, 39; 39:26)

It is by being confronted with these common grace works that Job repents in dust and ashes for his presumptuousness.

This leads to the second reason that giving thanks and praise to our Creator is so important. We know the Creator! We who have repented before God the Father by the work of Christ and through the regeneration of the Holy Spirit are those who may rightly offer up worship for common grace gifts.

Churches that have diluted, or even abandoned, the gospel of redemption pour their energy into common grace worship. God is praised for being Creator. He is thanked for the beauty of the earth and for the joy of human love. But the worship rings hollow. Christ, even if they use the term *Son of God*, is not honored as God. His life on earth and work on the cross are nothing more than moral examples. He has not turned us from enemies into righteous saints. We have never been cast out of the garden; never shut out from the Holy of Holies. We have always been able to give proper worship.

However nice the music may be, however friendly the worship leaders may seem, God the Creator and Ruler cannot be worshiped if he is not known as Redeemer. We cannot enter into his holy temple without first having been sprinkled with the blood of the Lamb. The Father accepts the praise of his adopted children, not of those who continue to reject his sentence of them and his salvation. We despise the thanks and compliments of hypocrites, especially of those who think we should be pleased with their self-admiration. In like manner the Creator disdains the worship of those who regard his gifts of common grace as common reward, which is the approach of churches that reject Christ's atoning work.

All the works of God shall praise his name; all the creatures named man ought to praise his name. But praise, to be accepted, is to come above all from his saints. "Oh come, let us worship and bow down; let us kneel before the Lord, our Maker! For he is our God, and we are the people of his pasture, and the sheep of his hand" (Ps. 95:6–7). Who are the "we" that worship and bow down before the Lord, our Maker? We who know him as our God because we have first acknowledged him as the "rock of our salvation" (v. 1).

Psalm 147 praises God, who "covers the heavens with clouds; he prepares rain for the earth; he makes grass grow on the hills. He gives to the beasts their food, and to the young ravens that cry" (vv. 8–9). These are common grace gifts, but the context of the psalm is that these gifts of God to the earth and its inhabitants are intended to encourage the covenant people of Jerusalem and Judah. And it is Jerusalem, the nation of Israel,

46

who knows God through his word (v. 19), who is able to recognize these common gifts as those of the great Yahweh. And so it is that the church, who through the Word of God knows the redemption of God, can now offer to him thanksgiving and praise worthy of his name. As Psalm 124:8 concludes, "Our help is in the name of the LORD, who made heaven and earth." Our help, our salvation, is in the name of the Lord who is Creator, who made heaven and earth. He is able to save because he is Creator. It is right for him to save because he is Creator. He saved us that we might acknowledge him as Creator.

To live and to worship in thanksgiving and praise to God as Creator and Provider is how it was meant to be. God created the world; he populated it with man and woman, who were to live in intimate relationship with their Creator. They were to be fruitful and to multiply, filling the earth with worshipers. They were to exercise dominion over the earth, living as stewards of God's rich bounty. Instead they rebelled, and their descendants did anything but give due thanks to their Creator. They went so far as to create their own "creators," or, as in our culture, to disavow that a creator even exists. God then, in his mercy, sent the redeemer Jesus Christ to ransom lost idolaters and to restore them as true worshipers of the true Creator.

Think of it this way. Suppose a father, who is also a doctor, has many children. They become infected with a deadly disease. Though they are near the point of death, he manages to save them with his medical knowledge. Those children grow up grateful to their father for saving their lives, and he is pleased with their thankfulness. But he had saved them not so he would win their gratitude for being saved, but that he may enjoy his relationship with them and they with him. He restored them to health that they might continue as a family. Likewise, God our Father restored us to a right relationship with him that we might live out lives of thankfulness and praise to him as our Father and Creator.

The weakness in this analogy is that our problem was not one of sickness but of rebellion, and that God did not need to save us in order to fulfill his role of being a father or to receive glory. His saving work was of grace and mercy, and it calls us to be ever thankful for such a salvation. Even so, we were saved that we might "proclaim the excellencies of him who called [us] out of darkness into his marvelous light" (1 Peter 2:9). We have come into the light that we may know our Father and may properly proclaim *all* his excellencies.

So we are to offer up sacrifices of thanksgiving for salvation and for what that salvation allows us to do—to give proper thanks to our Creator for his blessings of creation and of the gifts he gives indiscriminately to mankind. They are not lesser gifts—not to us who have received the gift of salvation.

Worship through Common Grace Means

Since God is Creator and Provider, not only may we extol him for what he has made and given, but we are to use those gifts and blessings for the purpose of glorifying him. We should think of worship in one sense as offering back to God what he has so graciously given to us. It can be difficult to strike the right balance in what we offer, but I would submit the following questions for consideration.

We know that what matters to God in worship is the heart.

And the LORD said:
"Because this people draw near with their mouth
    and honor me with their lips,
    while their hearts are far from me,
and their fear of me is a commandment taught by men,
therefore, behold, I will again
    do wonderful things with this people,
    with wonder upon wonder;
and the wisdom of their wise men shall perish,
    and the discernment of their discerning men shall be hidden." (Isa. 29:13–14)

48

Let us lift up our hearts and hands
　　to God in heaven. (Lam. 3:41)

Yes, what matters in worship, along with truth, is the condition and involvement of the heart. But I would ask, if we know God to be a God of beauty, if he has taken care to create not only a functional world but a beautiful world, if he has given ability to men and women to produce beautiful works and objects, should we not use those gifts and those resources to offer back to God beautiful worship? Is it not possible—even desirable—to express to God what is within our hearts through the external gifts he has graciously given to us in his common grace?

Evidently God does appreciate external beauty. There is, of course, his handiwork of creation. He designed a temple to be built and filled with the craft of artists. Jesus admired the beauty of the lilies. He accepted the costly ointment of Mary poured on his feet, calling the act a "beautiful thing" (Matt. 26:10). The heart matters, yes, but will not a person whose heart is filled with devotion and thanksgiving to God consider how to offer worship expressed through the beautiful gifts God has bestowed upon him? Are we not to consider how to express thanks to God through the physical gifts and the inner abilities that he has made common to mankind?

Or consider worship from the perspective of what impacts us. All of us have encountered physical scenes that inspired us to worship our Creator. Perhaps we climbed to a mountaintop or walked along a quiet beach. Perhaps we have been in open land on a cloudless night and beheld the starry sky. The mere experience of observing beauty lifted our hearts to be in awe of God, to sense his holiness, to glory in his beauty, to be filled with praise and thanksgiving. Should we not then give thought to the sanctuary that we enter into on the Lord's Day in order to give praise and thanksgiving to God for his holiness, his beauty, and his glory? Yes, what matters is our hearts, but if God seems to think that physical beauty impacts the heart, should we not give consideration to the structures in which we worship? Should we not use the gifts given by God to build and to craft surroundings that will inspire our hearts to worship? Should we not use natural talents in aiding our worship? Should we not make use of the gifts given to others to dress in a manner that aids us in worship?

We may still debate how much to spend on worship and what we should wear or how our sanctuaries should look, but what I am tackling is the notion that we can simply push aside such considerations by saying that God doesn't care about externals, that he only cares about the heart. What I want us to consider in our hearts is whether we are really speaking for God or for ourselves. Do we dress as we do for worship because we are convicted that God does not care about our appearance and does not want us to care, or is it because we just want to do our own thing, what makes us comfortable (not comfortable to worship, just comfortable)? We can dress out of pride, for sure, but we can also dress out of our own convenience. And yet we will buy and wear clothes that attract us because they were designed through common grace gifts to express beauty; we will buy and wear them for the purpose of expressing beauty, especially for "special" occasions. But then we give no thought to what we wear in worship to express our thanksgiving to God. We simply say that God cares only about the heart. We know that our clothes do affect how we feel. (At least those in the fashion business know this, however conscious or unconscious we may be of it.) Clothes may not make the man or the woman, but they do influence him or her. How do your clothes influence your appearing in the presence of God for worship with his people? Have you thought about it?

How does the appearance of your sanctuary influence you? Does walking into it help you to feel that you have come into the presence of God? How do the external forms of your worship service affect your heart's ability to "offer to God acceptable worship, with reverence and awe, for our God is a consuming fire" (Heb. 12:28–29)? Can you really say that externals do not matter, given that God has made us physical creatures and has given us common grace physical blessings and gifts that do inspire us and ennoble us?

Common grace teaches us that our Creator and Provider delights in external beauty. Why would he make what he takes no delight in? Did he mean for nature's beauty to delight only man and not himself? Did the wonders of the world and of the universe have to wait until man invented airplanes and submarines and spaceships before they could be appreciated?

Common grace also teaches us that God delights in the internal gifts he has given to regenerate and even unregenerate man for the purpose of expressing back that beauty. Can we believe that he is indifferent to the voice that he has granted to the singer, that he is indifferent to the skill of the musician or the artist or even the athlete who uses his gift to its fullest potential? Should not the children of God all the more take care to use their God-given gifts for his glory and to return thanks to him? Give thanks with a thankful heart, and let that thankful heart use the resources and gifts provided by God to fully express itself.

This is not a call to use all common grace gifts and means in worship—at least not in corporate worship. God does give instruction as to what is suitable. But again, it is a call not to simply dismiss external considerations when we decide how we are to give due thanks to God and how we are to stir up right feelings within ourselves.

In conclusion, we have considered how the doctrine of common grace informs us in our worship of God. It teaches us continually to recognize all God's good gifts and provisions as coming from our Creator and Provider. It teaches us that we ought continually to give thanks for these good gifts. It bids us to use God's good gifts to honor him in worship. It calls upon us who have been redeemed, who have been brought near to God as his covenant people, to lead the earth in giving thanks and praise to the Lord who created us all. So it is fitting to close with Psalm 148.

> Praise the LORD!
> Praise the LORD from the heavens;
>   praise him in the heights!
> Praise him, all his angels;
>   praise him, all his hosts!
>
> Praise him, sun and moon,
>   praise him, all you shining stars!
> Praise him, you highest heavens,
>   and you waters above the heavens!
>
> Let them praise the name of the LORD!
>   For he commanded and they were created.
> And he established them forever and ever;
>   he gave a decree, and it shall not pass away.
>
> Praise the LORD from the earth,
>   you great sea creatures and all deeps,
> fire and hail, snow and mist,
>   stormy wind fulfilling his word!
>
> Mountains and all hills,
>   fruit trees and all cedars!
> Beasts and all livestock,
>   creeping things and flying birds!
>
> Kings of the earth and all peoples,
>   princes and all rulers of the earth!
> Young men and maidens together,
>   old men and children!
>
> Let them praise the name of the LORD,
>   for his name alone is exalted;
>   his majesty is above earth and heaven.

He has raised up a horn for his people,
   praise for all his saints,
   for the people of Israel who are near to him.
Praise the Lord!

For Discussion

1. Can you name five common grace blessings for which to thank God?

2. Do you agree with the statement that "our problem is not what we lack but what we fail to see"? Looking back at today or yesterday, what did you fail to see?

3. What does the author mean by saying, "Thankfulness and praise are necessary to keep our hearts calibrated for proper worship and service to the only God, the only Giver of all good things"?

4. Do you ever pray a prayer purely of thanksgiving and praise, not asking God for anything? Try praying for five minutes without asking God to give you anything—including not asking him to make you more thankful.

5. How can knowing God as Redeemer overshadow knowing God as Creator?

6. How do we withhold from God his due by not acknowledging the "little" common grace blessings?

7. What does the author mean that only those who know God as Redeemer can worship God as Creator?

8. Do you agree or disagree that God takes an interest in external expressions of beauty and of reverence? Would you agree or disagree that in worship, thought should be given to external appearances?

| 4 |

Sharing the Gospel in Light of Common Grace

John Leonard

LAST YEAR my wife and I hosted a Saudi Arabian imam in our home for six months. Since we had worked with Muslims for ten years overseas, we jumped at the chance of having an imam live with us!

The experience wasn't at all what we were expecting. We thought that our Saudi guest would be withdrawn and distant, but he wasn't at all. He was a very personal and engaging young man in his early thirties. On occasion he would attend our community group and Bible study, and he never hurried to his room after meals but talked for long hours after supper. He would invite me to share a cup of Saudi coffee with him when I was home in the afternoons, and he actively participated in whatever the family was doing. Our Saudi guest was one of the most enjoyable people whom we have shared our home with, and such a deep bond has developed between us that he calls us his second mother and father.

Our Saudi friend was the epitome of what a good person should be. He was polite, courteous, and hospitable. In the time that he lived with us I did not see one hint of duplicity or hypocrisy. I did not see any hatred or animosity, but I saw someone who expressed a genuine tolerance and understanding of, and even love and concern for, others. Our guest could have been acting—but if he was, he was very, very good at it. In all honesty we enjoyed our Muslim guest much more than many Christian guests we have had in our home.

Over my lifetime I have had the privilege and even the real joy to know people from many different faiths, as well as people who confess no faith at all. I count Jews, Hindus, Buddhists, Baha'is, Wiccans, and nonreligious people as acquaintances and friends. What has impressed me with many of them is that they are the kind of people I would call to watch my children or leave a set of house keys with if we were going away. Many, from all outward appearances, seem to have marriages that are as strong as mine, to have children who are as well behaved and respectful as mine, and to enjoy life as much as I do. They are great neighbors and good friends. It appears from all outward indications that they don't need the gospel—they are doing just fine without Jesus, which some have even told me in one way or another.

Many Christians don't know people of other faiths, nor do they want to know any because getting to know them can be dangerous. But the danger isn't what we think it is—it isn't that they will convert us. The real danger is that we will get to know, like, and respect them. We may even conclude that people as good as these don't need the gospel at all. We may find ourselves questioning God's fairness as to why he would condemn to hell for all eternity people who are as good as, if not better than, we are. The end result is that God is blamed for all that is wrong with the world and mankind is credited with all that is good.

Understanding the biblical teaching on common grace can keep us from these errors. It is because of God's common grace and providence that people who worship other gods or no god at all can be really wonderful people and that so much in their lives, marriages, and families can be exemplary. Instead of questioning God's fairness we should be praising him for his goodness, because all the good in this world—and even the goodness in the people who deny him—is the active work of God's common grace.

People don't want to admit it, but our Creator is active in our world, bestowing his grace on all mankind so that most of life works for most people. The goodness that we see all around us in the daily acts of men should lead us to worship God because it proves that he is good. It should also motivate us to tell others about him and about their need to know and worship the One who has given them the daily blessings that they enjoy without recognizing him for it. The gospel is good news for all!

How then should we understand man's condition, God's character, Christ's work, the Spirit's ministry, and the gospel's glory in light of common grace when we share our hope?

Man's Condition

To forget or deny the doctrine of common grace causes us to misjudge the nature and character of mankind. One of the ways we do this is by demonizing non-Christians. There are two reasons we find it so easy to demonize them.

First, the doctrine of hell becomes more palatable if we believe that those who are going there are the worst kinds of people. Although the demonization of non-Christians may make it easier for us to accept that they rightly deserve their fate, the problem is that our demonization builds a false barrier between us and them, making sharing the gospel much more difficult because the caricature of them scares us. The demonization of others is the same technique that governments around the world use to turn their soldiers into killers. When we do the same thing with non-Christians, we will find it difficult to talk with or befriend them. We will not welcome them into our churches. They are the enemy! Instead of being the means through which people can come to faith, we become the very obstacles that keep them from hearing the gospel.

Secondly, we demonize non-Christians because it gives us a false security about the changes that the Lord has made in

our own lives. When we do this we look just like the Pharisee
in the parable who takes great comfort in not being like the tax
collector (see Luke 18). Like the Pharisee, we will see the worst in
people though it may not be there; we hope to look much better
because we are not like "that person." If we do bring ourselves
to speak to one of "those people," we often come off in a very
judgmental, self-righteous, and hypocritical way.

Once I was eating a large chocolate bar while standing next
to a man who was smoking. Concerned about his health, I told
him that he should stop smoking because it wasn't good for
him. He replied, "And your addiction to chocolate? Isn't that
just as bad?"

While he coughed on his smoke, I choked on my chocolate.
It was much easier to talk about this man's problems than to
talk "to him." One of the dangers in talking to non-Christians
is that they can see the hypocrisy in our lives as clearly as we
can see it in theirs.

The doctrine of common grace helps us to see people biblically. We know that anyone is capable of the greatest acts of
goodness and kindness—even of great love and sacrifice. But
this does not mean that we are good. It only means that we
have all been stamped with the indelible image of God from
creation, and that God's providence brings good out of that
which is broken.

In the encounter between Jesus and the rich ruler in Luke
18:18, a very "good" man comes to Christ wanting to know
whether he has been good enough to inherit eternal life. He
certainly seems to have all the outward signs that God favors
him. He is rich—being rich at that time and in that culture was
believed to be a sign of God's blessing on one's life. He is also
a ruler, proving that God favors him. Certainly one as good as
he must have earned or inherited eternal life. That would likely
be the overwhelming opinion of all who knew him.

There is no reason to doubt the answer that the ruler gives
to Jesus' response, "You know the commandments: 'Do not

commit adultery, Do not murder, Do not steal, Do not bear false witness, Honor your father and mother'" (Luke 18:20)—"All these I have kept from my youth" (Luke 18:21). "I've done that!" he is saying. He has done more than he has been asked to do. The statement "from my youth" could mean that before his bar mitzvah he was already keeping the law. For that he may hope that he has earned extra credit.

But what Jesus says to him he doesn't hear, and neither do we. For when this man addresses Jesus as "Good Teacher," Jesus responds, "Why do you call me good? No one is good except God alone" (Luke 18:19).

The ruler doesn't hear it because he doesn't stop to say, "Excuse me, did I hear you correctly? Did you say no one is good but God alone?" No—he, like most of us, hears only what he wants to hear and tells Jesus about his goodness. We don't want to hear Jesus' statement that "no one is good but God alone" because our question when we read Jesus' response is, "What is wrong with Jesus? Is he saying that he isn't good?"

What we don't want to hear is that we are not good. We, like the ruler, have a long list of accomplishments and we want them to count for something. Our goodness, like that of this ruler, has blinded us to our real need.

What we learn in the story of the rich ruler is that his goodness and our goodness aren't good enough, because Jesus tells us all, in the most graphic of descriptions using a camel and a needle, that salvation is beyond our ability. "For it is easier for a camel to go through the eye of a needle than for a rich person to enter the kingdom of God" (Luke 18:25).

Those who hear Jesus' statement are shocked! If this good man can't earn eternal life, or at least buy it, they are left to ask only, "Then who can be saved?" (Luke 18:26). Jesus' words seal any approach to God that is based on our efforts: "What is impossible with men is possible with God" (Luke 18:27). The truth is, our goodness isn't good enough.

The apostle Paul had the same problem. When it came to goodness Paul said he was "blameless" (Phil. 3:6). But he found out that his goodness was of no value whatsoever when it came to living in a right relationship with God. He concluded that his righteousness was only "garbage" (Phil. 3:8 NIV). In the Greek, the word means anything that is so detestable you immediately want to throw it away, like stinking dung.

We must not let the goodness of others keep us from sharing the hope of the gospel with them, because in reality trusting in that goodness is like trying to swim with an anchor. Instead of seeing man's great achievements as proof of his goodness, we should see them as evidence of the greatness that we were created for, and were once capable of, but from which we have fallen.

God's Character

Because of our nature we can misinterpret common grace. It can give us a false reading on our goodness and God's character. This happens when we measure ourselves against the wrong standard or are unaware of what the standard is.

I loved to run when I was younger. I ran twelve to fifteen miles a day and loved it. I believed that I had a talent for running and decided to prepare for running a marathon. I went to the library to do some research on running a marathon, and what I learned shocked me. I found out I was no runner at all. At best, I was a jogger at my eight to nine minute mile pace; real marathon runners were twice as fast as I was.

People have a similar problem when it comes to comparing their goodness with God's character. Because we don't want to understand the moral perfection of God and his holiness, we choose to compare ourselves to standards that make us appear to be much better than we are. The entire process causes us to focus on ourselves and not on our Creator—to change the standard and completely misread our condition. But it isn't that we just misread our own goodness, we also completely misunderstand it and will not give credit for that goodness where credit is due—to God.

What our goodness should teach us is that we have a Creator whose moral perfection and holiness transcend the goodness we see in the world around us. Our goodness can't even compare to his holiness.

This is seen most clearly when Isaiah has a vision of the Lord "high and lifted up" in the temple (Isa. 6:1). It is seen in two separate ways: the first is in the description of the angels, the six-winged seraphim who have from their creation been in the presence of God and are continually captivated by his holiness. These six-winged angels cover their heads and feet. The shocking thing about the description of these angels is that these perfect beings, compared to the majestic holiness of God, act as if they are the most unholy of creatures by covering themselves. In the presence of God all they can do is humbly worship.

The second is seen in the response of Isaiah, after he sees for the first time what the angels have beheld for ages. Isaiah, a prophet from out of whose mouth comes the very word of God, can only say when he has his vision of the Lord, in effect, "I have a filthy mouth!" Isaiah's response is repentance and obedience.

When we witness we often compare sin with the righteousness of God to show how poorly we live up to his standard. A better barometer would be to say that our goodness, when compared to God's holiness, is at best filthy rags (Isa. 64:6 NIV) and that the good that we do is the result of his common grace in our lives.

The evidence that our goodness isn't good enough is that we don't respond as either the angels or Isaiah did to our God—in repentance, worship, and obedience. This can be understood only when we comprehend the holiness of God.

The Work of Christ

When common grace is not recognized as the source of whatever goodness may be in us, we can diminish the nature and purpose of Christ's work on the cross. When we fool ourselves into believing that we are good enough, it causes us to look at Christ's death on the cross as either an inspiring example we should attempt to follow or, at worst, a tragedy in which Christ was a victim who died a needless death. What we do not want to admit is what the Scriptures teach, "That Christ Jesus came into the world to save sinners" (1 Tim. 1:15).

By shedding his blood Christ was able to do what common grace can never do—fully satisfy the holy God whom we have offended. Paul speaks of Christ's work as settling a debt we cannot pay. To the Colossians he writes, "Having forgiven us all our trespasses, by canceling the record of debt that stood against us with its legal demands. This he set aside, nailing it to the cross" (Col. 2:13–14).

Christ not only satisfies our debts with God, he delivers us from the power of the evil one by the cross. Again in Colossians 2 Paul states that Christ has won a total victory. "He disarmed the rulers and authorities and put them to open shame, by triumphing over them" (v. 15).

Christ not only removed the curse we are under and delivered us from the power of Satan, he made us alive through his resurrection. Paul explains to the Colossians, "And you, who were dead in your trespasses and the uncircumcision of your flesh, God made alive together with him" (Col. 2:13).

Common grace can never compare to the perfect and finished work of Christ.

The Ministry of the Spirit

Common grace and providence should not be confused with the ministry of the Spirit. The Holy Spirit applies to the lives of his people the benefits won by Christ's work of uniting us with Christ. It is out of union with Christ that all the benefits are ours. These benefits can be looked at in two ways: there are those that unite us to Christ and those that conform us to his image. One benefit that unites us to Christ is regeneration.

This is the first work that God does through the Holy Spirit in the lives of his people. It precedes repentance and faith, which is our response to what the Spirit has done in our lives. When Jesus told Nicodemus he must be born again (John 3:3), he links that work to the Spirit of God in John 3:5: "Unless one is born of water and the Spirit."

Common grace, by either its presence or its absence, is not an indicator of the Holy Spirit's saving work in someone. We should proclaim the gospel to everyone, regardless of the evidence of God's common grace in their lives.

A second work of the Spirit is to conform us to Christ's image. Everything in our lives is transformed by the work of the Spirit so that our lives are different from the lives of the people around us. This too is the work of the Spirit whereby he produces in us the qualities that are seen in God the Father and God the Son.

In Paul's letter to the Galatians he writes about the fruit that the Spirit of God produces in our lives, which no law or work of man apart from the Spirit's work in us can ever produce. It is important to note that this fruit is in the singular, but has nine dimensions: "love, joy, peace, patience, kindness, goodness, faithfulness, gentleness, self-control" (Gal. 5:22–23). Fruit, in the singular, teaches us that all these dimensions should be seen in our lives—not just a few.

Most Christians are committed to "friendship evangelism." By this I mean that a foundation of friendship is laid with a non-Christian. The problem I have with this approach is that throughout our friendships we never demonstrate anything more than those qualities that are the result of common grace. The love, joy, peace, patience, kindness, goodness, faithfulness, gentleness, and self-control is qualitatively no better than what a non-Christian gives us back in return. Could our poor results in friendship evangelism be because there doesn't seem to be anything special in the way we live out our Christian lives? That our lives don't conform to the character of our Lord?

The Gospel's Glory

The doctrine of God's common grace should also teach us something of the special grace that is offered only in the gospel, because they are related in at least two ways.

First, as God's common grace touches and impacts every aspect of everyone's life, the gospel in which Christ offers saving grace to his people leavens every part of our lives. There is no area of a Christian's life that is not changed by God's saving grace. It cannot be hemmed in or restrained to a couple of areas of our lives. If it is, then it's not God's special grace at work. Paul tells us in 2 Corinthians 5:17, "If anyone is in Christ, he is a new creation. The old has passed away; behold, the new has come."

The glory of the gospel is that it doesn't transform only those areas of our lives that we believe need changing. It also transforms those areas of our lives that we are not even aware need changing, and it even pries our hands off those areas of our lives that we don't want Christ to touch at all. The way that you know Christ is at work in your life is because he messes with *everything*.

We have sold the gospel to people as quick help for a particular problem rather than as a complete makeover that will last a lifetime. The glory of the gospel is that it is not patchwork—it is a new creation.

Secondly, just as God's common grace is manifested in the physical world, impacting people's lives and society as a whole, God's special grace spills over our personal lives, manifesting itself in relationships, families, communities, cultures, and the world. I call this phenomenon "turning the world right-side up." This is based on the response of the Thessalonians, who in Acts 17:6 describe Paul's missionary team as "these men who have turned the world upside down."

The glory of the gospel is that it manifests itself by bringing together people from very diverse backgrounds, cultures, and socioeconomic groups and makes them into a new community—a new humanity and kingdom that the Bible calls the church.

Together we cannot help bumping into the world around us, leaving it changed by the grace that God has given us. The glory of the gospel is that it results in a community of people who live out together the truth of everything the gospel promises, becoming the place where heaven touches earth and where the promises of God are experienced in the life of the community. There is no better way to share the gospel than to invite non-Christians to be a part of that community.

The glory of the gospel is also seen in how it does what common grace cannot do. God's special grace reconciles us through Christ with our heavenly Father. There is a heavenly dimension to the gospel. The gospel is more than a message about how to be good people; it is a call to repentance and to live in a right relationship with God.

We have sold the gospel short by making its message secular, about only life in this world. We have done so hoping to generate interest among secular people, but all we have done by presenting a one-dimensional gospel is given people the impression that they don't need it.

A secular gospel is one that promises Jesus will improve the quality of your life here on earth—that he can make your marriage, family, and personal life more fulfilling. The problem is that many people are happy with the condition of their lives and don't feel as if they have any need of the gospel that promises only to improve life for them here on earth.

When we were working with Muslims in France there was a young woman who was doing everything she could to please God. She wanted with all her heart to serve Allah. She was a very moral and religious person. She demonstrated these characteristics in her life by her concern for others. She was a very hardworking young lady, but she still made time in the midst of her studies for helping whoever was in need.

When we met her she would have said that she was perfectly happy and content with who she was and with the religion in which she was raised. One afternoon a Moroccan Christian came by to see her in her dorm room and shared Christ with her. This was the first time she had heard about Jesus. It wasn't out of her felt need that she embraced Christ, but it was the beauty of Christ that drew her to him.

We must stop selling the gospel as the "little more" in life that people are lacking. The glory of the gospel is that it sets right the fundamental relationship in our lives, our relationship with God. That is our real need, whether we know it or not.

The glory of the gospel is unlike God's common grace because the special grace of Christ can bring comfort and hope to the most troubled heart. In Luke 19 we find Zacchaeus hoping to get a look at Jesus. Zacchaeus knew that his real problem was not his physical height but his spiritual condition. He came up short when it came to measuring up to God's standards.

It wasn't that Zacchaeus was an evil man as far as men go, but that he was tainted by his occupation. As a tax collector he was outside the covenant people. First, he was part of a profession whose members had a reputation of being thieves. A tax collector was considered to be one whether he was or not. Secondly, he was collaborating with the enemy. Zacchaeus was working for Rome and was therefore a traitor to his people. Thus, everyone who dealt with Zacchaeus was a continual reminder that he was not part of the people of God—the nation of Israel. Common grace offered him no hope, but Christ found him.

No matter what Zacchaeus and others believed to be the obstacles that kept him from being in a right relationship with God, these were not obstacles for Christ. In the story of Zacchaeus, Christ proved not only that he came to seek and to save the lost, but also that he actually can and does find and save even those whom all of society writes off as being beyond the reach of God's grace. The glory of the gospel is that the opinion of men is not the opinion of Christ. For Christ declared that even this tax collector was a "son of Abraham" and that "salvation has come to this house" (Luke 19:9).

Paul, Acts, and Common Grace

How may common grace be used to evangelize? There are two passages in Acts in which Paul uses common grace as a bridge to sharing the gospel: Acts 14, where Paul and Barnabas are in Lystra and are mistaken for Zeus and Hermes, and Acts 17, where Paul is addressing the philosophers at the Areopagus in Athens. In these two accounts, is Paul giving us an example of a method that we should use to share our faith with those who do not know the God of the Bible?

There are several problems with using either of these accounts as a model for evangelism. The first is that Luke tells us so little of the actual words spoken by Paul—there are just three verses in Acts 14 and ten verses in Acts 17. These are the only two instances in which Luke records Paul using this method, so with such little evidence it is difficult to render a verdict about standardizing Paul's approach.

Second, Paul was not successful in either Lystra or Athens, if you measure success by the planting of a church. In Lystra Paul was stoned and in Athens he was mocked by some. We are not told that anyone was converted in Lystra, although in Acts 16:1 we are told that Timothy was from Lystra. However, we are not absolutely sure—Timothy could have been from Derbe, a city near Lystra (see Acts 20:4, where Paul, listing friends, writes, "Gaius of Derbe, and Timothy"). In Athens we learn that some men believed (Acts 17:34). But was their faith a result of Paul's address on the Areopagus, or because he "reasoned in the synagogue with the Jews and the devout persons, and in the marketplace every day with those who happened to be there" (Acts 17:17)?

Ten times in Acts the word *reasoned* is used, but only in Acts 19–24. Luke uses *preached* fourteen times when describing Paul's work in Acts 9–17, but only once after that in Acts 20:7 (KJV). Does this change of terms represent a change in the content of Paul's message or a change in the way Paul interacted with his audience? The word for *reasoned* in the Greek can be transliterated as "dialogue." From how Luke describes Paul's work, it seems that the change was one more of method than of message. Luke writes, "Disputing and persuading the things concerning the kingdom of God" (Acts 19:8 KJV) and "All they which dwelt in Asia heard the word of the Lord Jesus, both Jews and Greeks" (Acts 19:10 KJV). Paul makes clear his consistent message in 1 Corinthians 2:2, where he states, "For I decided to know nothing among you except Jesus Christ and him crucified" (KJV).

Third, Paul changes his missionary strategy after he leaves Athens. Before coming to Athens, Paul moves quickly from town to town, perhaps staying a few weeks, at most a month, in one place. After Athens, he stays for a year and a half in Corinth (Acts 18:11) and is in Ephesus for at least two years (Acts 19:10). Could it be that Paul was learning that it takes time to teach those who have had little contact with God's Word and who thus need a much longer time to understand and embrace the gospel?

It is not clear from the two times in Acts when Paul uses common grace as a bridge to the gospel whether this should be our "method" for sharing the gospel with non-Christians. In my experience of sharing my faith, it is best to begin with what we may have in common. With a Muslim that may be a desire to know and serve God or the disappointment over sin. When I am in discussion with a Muslim, instead of arguing over every point, I will not challenge some statements he makes. For example, when a Muslim says we worship the same God, I will let that pass because I don't want to get into the details of how the Muslim God and the Christian God differ. There is usually plenty of time for those discussions if the person is truly interested in knowing what Christians believe.

At some point you must step beyond what you and the other person have in common in order to challenge that individual with the claims of the gospel. It is a mistake to believe that the more time you spend agreeing with someone on common grace issues the easier it is to cross over to the demands of the gospel.

We need more than an intellectual connection through long discussions about what we agree on, and we need more than an emotional connection through a long friendship in which we hope that our lives have proven the truth of the gospel. We need the Spirit of God to awaken the hearts and minds of individuals. Paul's work in Lystra and Athens proves that.

Common grace is not *special* or *saving* grace! If you choose to use common grace as a bridge to the gospel, be sure that the bridge connects over to the other side of the gospel bank. Common grace needs to take everyone to repentance. That was Paul's intent when he told the Athenians, "The times of ignorance God overlooked, but now he commands all people everywhere to repent" (Acts 17:30). It is the same warning that Paul gives in his letter to the Romans.

> Or do you presume on the riches of his kindness and forbearance and patience, not knowing that God's kindness is meant to lead you to repentance? But because of your hard and impenitent heart you are storing up wrath for yourself on the day of wrath when God's righteous judgment will be revealed. (Rom. 2:4–5)

The unregenerates' misapplication about common grace is that the more blessings they receive from it, the less "felt need" they have of God. Whatever your starting point may be, be sure to take your hearer to the gospel and to pray for God's special grace to grant open ears and an open heart.

For Discussion

1. According to the author, a Christian may demonize unregenerate neighbors for what reasons? How does having a biblical understanding of man's condition allow us to accept the goodness we see in our neighbors?

2. How does a recognition of the holiness of God put man's goodness into proper perspective?

3. How does Christ's work on the cross put man's goodness into proper perspective?

4. How can common grace gifts in our neighbors mislead us in understanding their true spiritual condition?

5. What is the necessary work of the Holy Spirit in salvation?

6. What does the author mean by the statement, "We have sold the gospel short by making its message secular, about only life in this world"? Do you agree or disagree?

7. How may common grace be used as a bridge for evangelism? What are its limits?

Common Grace and
Loving Your Neighbor

Ruth Naomi Floyd

BOBBY WAS THRASHING around in the hospital bed. He was conscious and his groaning was unbearable. His eyes haunted me; they were filled with fear, suffering, and rage. Bobby desperately wanted relief. The morphine had ceased working and the doctors were unable to provide further medical assistance. Months leading up to Bobby's last hospitalization were spent preparing for his passing. We prayed for a peaceful and quiet death and had faith that God would hear our prayers and have mercy.

As someone who worked with those suffering from HIV/AIDS, I often had the privilege of accompanying patients as they walked through the final season of their lives. Though one never grows accustomed to watching a human being pass away, there was something about Bobby's death that was profoundly different. I had never experienced a death characterized by such terrifying anguish. The physicians were frustrated. They recommended that everyone, both family and friends, leave the hospital room until it was over.

I refused to leave.

I had made a promise to Bobby that if at all possible, I would be present with him as the end drew near. His worst fear was dying alone. I kept my promise and watched and waited, but there was no peace for Bobby in the end. His last breath was filled with tremendous suffering.

My heart was broken when Bobby's family reentered the room. His face was contorted, his body twisted. God had not answered Bobby's prayer, nor my own. I was overcome with sorrow and disappointment. I believed in God's sovereignty. I believed that God could do whatever he wanted—where, when, and however he chose. His will was holy. Perfect. Who was I to question it? Yet I couldn't dismiss my overwhelming grief at what I had witnessed. All I could do was to give thanks that Bobby was a strong believer in Jesus Christ. His suffering was finally over, and he was now standing in the presence of his Lord, free of pain, anguish, and death. This alone brought comfort.

The following week another patient named Ed was going through the final stages of AIDS, and being close to death, he asked me to sit with him while he waited for his relatives to arrive. Like Bobby, he did not desire to die alone.

It surprised me how comfortable his private hospital room was, filled with an abundance of flowers, cards, and gifts. During the previous nine months my interactions with Ed had been challenging and marked with frustration. Ed had been a proud, self-proclaimed racist and atheist. He hated God, even as he denied his very existence. Yet here I was, waiting with him at the final curtain. Though he expressed dismay in regard to the inevitability of his situation and impending death, he was grateful not to be in pain. We waited together for many hours while his family faced delays on the highway.

In the months leading up to this moment, never a day went by when Ed had not cracked a racial joke or uttered racial slurs in my hearing. But now, in and out of sleep, this surly man of many harsh words could barely speak. With his tired, weak, and feeble voice, Ed told me that he had not changed his views on God, and that he would remain an atheist forever.

The next morning when Ed took his final breath, it was the most beautiful death I had ever witnessed. He died with a little smile on his face. Within a few moments of his death the sun came out from behind thick gray clouds and ushered in lovely beams of light. It was extremely tranquil. I waited there with him until his family arrived. They were grateful that Ed spent his last hours of life resting pain-free in a quaint room with a beautiful window view. I left the hospital grateful that Ed and his relatives had not had the horrific experience that Bobby and his relatives had gone through only the week before.

Why did God allow Bobby, a kind and loving man who had a strong Christian faith, to die such a horrific death while Ed, who rejected God and was unkind, died an absolutely serene and peaceful death?

However difficult it remains to understand such suffering for the believer, the goodness shown to Ed can be found in the doctrine of God's common grace. God's common grace restrains sin. It restrains his wrath. God's common grace provides many blessings and extends to all mankind. This grace is for all who embrace Christ and his cross, yet those who reject Christ and his cross partake of it as well. God's common grace was lavished on both Bobby and Ed during their lives and was even present during their deaths. I was commanded to love Bobby and Ed regardless of whether we were friends or enemies. Jesus says,

> You have heard that it was said, "You shall love your neighbor and hate your enemy." But I say to you, Love your enemies and pray for those who persecute you, so that you may be sons of your Father who is in heaven. For he makes his sun rise on the evil and on the good, and sends rain on the just and on the unjust. For if you love those who love you, what reward do you have? Do not even the tax collectors do the same? And if you greet only your brothers, what more are you doing than others? Do not even the Gentiles do the same? (Matt. 5:43–47)

Here Jesus explains the inner workings of God's common grace while also exhorting us to live it out. As God allows the sun to rise on the just and the unjust, so we are supposed to extend love, grace, and mercy to both friends and enemies. God gets the glory when we love those who do not love us, because it demonstrates how his redemptive love works toward us: "while we were yet sinners, Christ died for us" (Rom. 5:8 KJV). Our response to Christ's sacrificial love toward us on the cross is to love our neighbors and our enemies, showing no partiality, as our good works point back to our Savior while bringing many sons to glory.

Who exactly are our neighbors? Are neighbors merely those persons who reside in the same geographical location—community, city, state, or nation? Are neighbors those who share the same religion, spiritual beliefs, morals, values, and theology? Do neighbors share a common history, race, experience, or cultural identity? What about persons who love those of their same gender—are they considered neighbors of those who do not share that lifestyle? Can persons living within various socioeconomic brackets still be considered neighbors though they are separated by class? Are the outsiders and outcasts of society our neighbors?

The answer is yes. The vast array of global humanity falls under the umbrella of neighborhood. As Christians we are to show and extend love to every human being created and designed by God. If we truly believe that God created mankind in his own image, then we should not recreate human beings into images that make us feel more comfortable or that are deemed more acceptable. We must be willing to fully see and accept their God-given humanity.

After loving God, we are commanded to love our neighbors (Mark 12:30–31). Jesus has gone before us, telling us and showing us how to love. In order to actively love our neighbors, we must be willing to have the posture of a servant. We cannot love if we refuse to see our neighbors' true humanity, regardless of whether we agree or disagree with their choices, beliefs, or lifestyles. However, extending love does not mean that we compromise on the standards of God's Word. We can truly love our neighbors only as long as elitism, racism, sexism, homophobia, transphobia, and misogyny are purged from our hearts. We are called to love, not to tolerate. This distinction is crucial to loving and understanding our neighbors fully and organically. In his book *Holy Subversion: Allegiance to Christ in an Age of Rivals* author Trevin Wax states,

> We are not merely called to tolerate those who disagree with us; we are called to love. The world's idea of tolerance is a parody of the Christian understanding of love. Tolerance is passive. Love is active. Tolerance is a feeling of apathy. Love is accompanied by feelings of great affection. Tolerance keeps people at arm's length in hopes of not offending them. Love embraces people where they are and "hopes all things." Tolerance leaves people alone as individuals. Love ushers people into a community of generosity. Tolerance keeps a safe distance between those in need. Love rolls up its sleeves in service even to those who may be unlikeable. Tolerance avoids confrontation in order to maintain "peace." Love tells the truth boldly and graciously in order to bring about a deeper, more lasting peace.[1]

We should be willing not only to give love, but actually to become an act of love. We should make ourselves available to those who need grace, not merely tolerate their existence. If we can be willing to listen and serve, this form of love ultimately transcends self-interests and focuses on the expression of agape. Giving the gift of love to our neighbors means fully and freely giving of ourselves without expecting any acknowledgment or affirmation in return.

However, it remains true that though it is one thing to love those who are radically different from us (our neighbors), it is another thing entirely to love our enemies, those who deliberately seek to hurt and harm us. Here is how our Lord addresses this more challenging enactment of agape love:

> Love your enemies, do good to those who hate you, bless those who curse you, pray for those who abuse you. To one who strikes you on the cheek, offer the other also, and from one who takes away your cloak do not withhold your tunic either. Give to everyone who begs from you, and from one who takes away your goods do not demand them back. And as you wish that others would do to you, do so to them.
>
> If you love those who love you, what benefit is that to you? For even sinners love those who love them. And if you do good to those who do good to you, what benefit is that to you? For even sinners do the same. And if you lend to those from whom you expect to receive, what credit is that to you? Even sinners lend to sinners, to get back the same amount. But love your enemies, and do good, and lend, expecting nothing in return, and your reward will be great, and you will be sons of the Most High, for he is kind to the ungrateful and the evil. Be merciful, even as your Father is merciful. (Luke 6:27–36)

Anyone who harbors ill will can be characterized as an enemy. As part of the fabric of mankind, our enemies, like our neighbors, are made in the image of God. In this way enemies are merely a subcategory of the larger category called "neighbor." Jesus commands us to love our enemies and to do good toward them. This is a hard commandment to obey. But, as Saint Augustine writes, "If you believe what you like in the gospels and reject what you don't like, it is not the gospel you believe, but yourself."[2] Though it is not natural or easy to love our enemies, it is what God often ordains for our own sanctification and is a witness of his grace and redemption.

Loving our enemies means not wavering in obedience; it is our posture toward obeying this commandment and all God's commandments that accurately reveals what is truly in our own hearts. This area of our lives is one way in which our faith is tested and refined. Our enemies hold mirrors up for us to see the true reflection of our hearts. The presence of enemies is part of God's sovereign plan to strengthen, grow, and transform us. They are unwitting participants in helping us to die to ourselves as we reach for the One who chose to love us and die for us—we who were his enemies. As the apostle Paul explains in his letter to the Romans,

> For while we were still weak, at the right time Christ died for the ungodly. For one will scarcely die for a righteous person—though perhaps for a good person one would dare even to die—but God shows his love for us in that while we were still sinners, Christ died for us. (Rom. 5:6–8)

Often, we confuse loving our enemies with keeping the peace and avoiding confrontation. But, as the Word states, it is not enough to restrain ourselves and ignore the sins committed against us. We need to actively pursue agape love toward the transgressor. We cannot escape or hide from this commandment. We are called to obey with integrity and compassion, willing good for those who would will us ill. In spite of the evil thoughts, hurtful words, unkind actions, and vicious attacks from our enemies, our responses should always reflect God's love.

The transformation we go through as we rest in God's grace when dealing with our enemies is a witness of the gospel. We cannot show grace, forgiveness, patience, and loving-kindness toward anyone without first recognizing and affirming how the Lord has chosen to deal with our own sin against him. It is only from the outpouring of our gratitude for the forgiveness of our sins against the Son of Man, which we experience through the gospel, that we can ever forgive those around us who hurt us. It is for the sake of the gospel that we walk in obedience in this area, so that many will see our good deeds and glorify the Father in heaven (see Matt. 5:16).

This is why we are commanded to pray for our enemies. We must pray for strength to endure as well as for wisdom, discernment, and protection. We must also pray that our enemies' hearts will be changed and softened—that the Holy Spirit may peel back the layers of hostility and animosity. Even so, we must ask in prayer that God will grant us a Christlike attitude when we deal with those who hurt us, even if their hearts are not changed. We must ask for patience and grace so that his love will be manifested in us for the sake of his glory. Our love for our neighbors and our enemies should reflect the love of God. Christ has gone before us:

> Prepare me one body,
> I'll go down, I'll go down.
> Prepare me one body like man;
> I'll go down and die.
> The man of sorrows, sinner, see
> I'll go down, I'll go down,
> He died for you and he died for me
> I'll go down and die.[3]

He endured and conquered the cross, death, hell, and the grave. It is finished! Jesus' sacrificial gift of himself offered up in obedience for our salvation demonstrates amazing grace, and when we repent of our sins and embrace this grace we are saved. It is this same profound, unfathomable grace that requires us to love our neighbors. When we who have been chosen remember the love displayed on the cross at Calvary, we are able to truly love our neighbors as Jesus commands us, and we are transformed into instruments that he uses to bring forth common grace in the lives of others. As Christians, are we willing to submit to God's will in this area?

I am not suggesting the old adage "Love the sinner and hate the sin," but we are called to give the gift of love. Loving your neighbors does not mean judging their actions, choices, or lifestyles. It means meeting them where they are. Our motivation is to glorify God and to be vessels of his mercy and common grace. Though we pray that those around us will see Christ reflected in the love we give, and though we hope that the Holy Spirit will draw them nigh unto Christ, our commandment is to love. John 13:34–35 reads,

> So now I am giving you a new commandment: Love each other. Just as I have loved you, you should love each other. Your love for one another will prove to the world that you are my disciples. (NLT)

To accomplish this, we have to come out of our insular Christian communities. We must push aside our comfort level and be willing to love our neighbors and allow Christ to shine through us. It means we have to make ourselves accessible—to all peoples. Why? Because Christ made himself accessible to us.

> Jesus! What a friend for sinners!
> Jesus! Lover of my soul;
> Friends may fail me, foes assail me,
> He, my Savior, makes me whole.
>
> Jesus! I do now receive him,
> More than all in him I find.
> He hath granted me forgiveness,
> I am his, and he is mine.
>
> Hallelujah! What a Savior!
> Hallelujah! What a friend!
> Saving, helping, keeping, loving,
> He is with me to the end.[4]

Jesus understands what it means to love in the face of hurt, harm, and evil. He knows what it means to love enemies in the face of death. Jesus commands us to give the love that is rooted in him and based on his grace, even as it brings forth sanctification and promotes change within our own hearts. God allows our enemies to be that refining fire as he conforms us to the image of Christ. Every time we choose love over hate, we die a little more to self and change is wrought in our own lives as well as in the lives of those around us. He is perfecting us as we strive toward holiness and submit to his will. Though it may not appear to be the case in our temporal circumstances, we are never defeated when we follow Christ's commandments and walk in his footsteps. We carry the cross with great faith, knowing that he will never forsake us or leave us alone. Listen to these words of comfort from Isaiah:

> But now thus says the LORD,
> He who created you, O Jacob,
>   He who formed you, O Israel:
> "Fear not, for I have redeemed you;
>   I have called you by name, you are mine.
> When you pass through the waters, I will be with you;
>   and through the rivers, they shall not overwhelm you;
> when you walk through fire you shall not be burned,
>   and the flame shall not consume you." (Isa. 43:1–2)

Israel had been spiritually blind, rebellious, and filled with sin. They deserved God's judgment and wrath, but God showed mercy and chose to restore and redeem them. In the passage above, he reminds Israel that he created and formed them. He affirms his love to Israel. With this love, God provides words of comfort. He instructs his chosen not to be afraid of the hardships ahead and he calls them by name and rescues them. Israel is assured that they belong to the Lord in spite of their sin, and God claims them for his own. God does not promise the absence of suffering, but he assures their deliverance. The waters and rivers will not overwhelm his chosen ones. Israel shall not be consumed by flame, but they will be redeemed and brought home.

The God of Israel was not blind to the chosen nation's circumstances, nor is he blind to our own sufferings. His commands and promises speak directly to them. When we obey the Lord in loving our enemies, often we will suffer. We will endure pain, loss, affliction, and grief. But he says, "When you pass through the waters, I will be with you; and through the rivers, they shall not overwhelm you; when you walk through fire you shall not be burned, and the flame shall not consume you." Will you pass through the waters? Will you pass through fire and flames? God's promises provide the hope and strength we need to endure. The Ancient of Days created and formed us! He says, "Fear not, for I have redeemed you; I have called you by name, you are mine." The One who calls us by name will never leave us or forsake us, but he will complete that which he began in us. The path of love will be well worth it when we see him in all his glory. Bobby knows this, and we will too one day.

Bobby was my neighbor. When we met, he was deeply depressed. Bobby's health was declining and he was all alone. He was estranged from his family and friends and he desperately wanted to reconcile with them. At our weekly visits Bobby talked openly and honestly about his life. He was born into a Christian family who loved and supported him. After college he entered a successful career, married, and had two children. He was healthy and happy.

During travel for his job Bobby started drinking and hanging out at bars. He became an alcoholic and started engaging in anonymous sexual activities. This lifestyle began affecting Bobby's marriage and performance at work. He eventually was fired from his job and his wife took the children and left him. For several years Bobby went through a downward spiral out of control and eventually became destitute. After being hospitalized for a bad accident, he was diagnosed with full-blown AIDS. Toward the end of his life, Bobby's main goal was to be reconciled to his family. Though he made a childhood profession of faith the gospel never took hold, as he understood Christ to be a righteous judge who sought to punish his children. Bobby had never fully comprehended God's love and mercy.

As our friendship deepened we started to have more conversations about his life, and one day Bobby asked me if I would explain to him the doctrine of grace. He was amazed and could not believe that God would forgive all the wrong he had done. This was not the Jesus he had grown used to fearing and dreading. Bobby embraced God's forgiveness and grace in Jesus Christ and began faithfully studying the Scriptures while going to church when his health allowed. He loved studying the Word of God and enjoyed singing the hymns of the faith.

As the months passed, Bobby's health began to deteriorate at a fast pace. We began planning for his death and praying that he would be reconciled with his family. Bobby had enormous faith that God would answer his prayers. He always ended his prayers with, "Not my will but your will, O Lord." After he made many unsuccessful attempts to reconcile with his family, the Lord answered his prayers and he was restored to those relationships.

Bobby's last hospitalization lasted for over three weeks. It was a long and painful time for him. Bobby was fearful but had great faith that God would give him a peaceful death. God did not answer Bobby's prayer. His death was terrible.

I learned many things from my friendship with Bobby. I am blessed by his life and testimony. Bobby's profound gratefulness for God's redemptive love was convicting and it greatly encouraged my own walk. Like all of us, Bobby rebelled, but God in his great mercy called him by name and restored and redeemed him. In the midst of his great suffering and a terrible death, God called him home. Charles Spurgeon states,

> I tell you again, if there be any pathway in which there be not fire, tremble, but if your lot be hard, thank God for it. If your sufferings be great, bless the Lord for them, and if the difficulties in your pathway be many, surmount them by faith, but let them not cast you down. Be of good courage, and wait on the Lord, setting this constantly in your minds that he has not promised to keep you from trouble, but to preserve you in

it. It is not written, "I will save thee from the fire," but "I will save thee in the fire," not "I will quench the coals," but "they shall not burn thee," not "I will put out the furnace," but "the flames shall not kindle upon thee."[5]

Ed was my enemy. We were stuck with each other. Ed did not believe in the existence of God. He also did not believe that all human beings were created equal. Ed came to our HIV/AIDS ministry out of pure desperation. He was dying. He needed assistance in his preparation to meet death.

At first I was excited about the challenge that our relationship presented. My motivation was to help him to see and accept Jesus as his Savior and change his racist views. For the first three months I was energetic, positive, and hopeful. Ed wore me down. Our times together were filled with layers of tension. I struggled to go out of my way to give Ed the gift of love. The reality was that, at best, I was showing him false acts of love. At first glance my good works looked authentic. I thought I was doing an excellent job of trying to shield my dislike for Ed. However, my heart revealed my true emotions. I came to dread our time together. He was unappreciative and critical of everything I did to help him. I was discouraged.

One day, as I was praying, the Lord showed me my heart. I was ashamed and grieved. I did not love Ed; I tolerated him. My kind words and deeds were lies. My heart was hardened and angry toward Ed. I cried out to the Lord to change my heart. I asked him to help me to love Ed—through everything. I confessed my sins and asked for wisdom and strength. When I later met with Ed, I confessed how I had sinned against him and I asked for forgiveness. He did not accept my apology. He instead held it over my head. However, God answered my prayers and I did grow to love Ed. God had transformed my heart even though there had not been any change in Ed's heart. I continued to pray for both of us. I'm not saying that any of this was easy. It is hard to give love and have it rejected.

Over the next three months, Ed taught me many things about life, death, and human nature. When Ed took his last breath he clung tightly to his beliefs. In that moment I wept. I wept because Ed had not embraced the gospel of Jesus Christ. I wept because Ed had rejected the love I offered. I wept because God had allowed my relationship with Ed to reveal a deeper understanding of the daily love, mercy, and amazing grace that God daily extends toward me. I wept because of God's common grace.

When I find myself doubting God and being unkind to my fellow humans, I remember Ed and realize that in eternity's eyes, the only difference between myself and others is the redeeming, saving grace of the gospel of Jesus Christ.

To be servants of the Most High King we must be willing to obey, relinquish, and love. The path of pain and suffering is part of the trail to deliverance and our eternal home. What did I learn from Bobby's and Ed's deaths? I learned many things.

Bobby's suffering was great until his last breath. God delivered Bobby. The Creator and Redeemer of Bobby called him by name. Bobby passed through the waters, and God was with him. Bobby passed through the rivers, but they did not sweep over him. Bobby walked through the fire, but he was not burned; the flames did not set him ablaze. He was not consumed but was delivered to eternal joy with his Savior, Deliverer, Healer, and God. No more waters of pain. No more rivers of suffering. No more fires of grief. No more flames of loss.

Ed's death was beautiful, but once he drew his last breath he never experienced peace and joy again. He walked through the water and drowned. He walked through the fire and flames and was consumed. Ed was not delivered.

Because of our sin we deserve Ed's fate, but by God's grace, mercy, and love he made a way for our sin to be paid on the cross. Jesus paid it all. When we embrace Christ and his cross, we take up our cross, become servants of love, and follow Christ.

For Discussion

1. Is it troubling to you that the Christian in this story died a painful death and the atheist a peaceful death?

2. What is the distinction that the author makes between love and tolerance?

3. Which "neighbors" are the most difficult for you to love? Why?

4. What does the author mean by the statement, "The presence of enemies is part of God's sovereign plan to strengthen, grow and transform us"? How does that work?

5. Though Bobby had been raised in a Christian home, what doctrine had he failed to grasp?

6. Do you know of "Christians" who nevertheless are burdened by thinking that their salvation depends on works-righteousness?

7. Was the author's love for Ed wasted love because Ed did not repent and turn to Christ? How does the doctrine of common grace come into play with the answer?

6

How Should We Then Live in the World?

David Skeel

THREE DECADES AGO, two college girls spent the summer
before their senior year working with the migrant farm workers
who harvest lettuce, tomatoes, and other crops in rural North
Carolina. The girls helped to coordinate first aid, legal support,
and other services for the workers, most of whom came from
Central America. They slept in the same wooden shacks that the
workers lived in. They didn't exactly take a vow of poverty, but
it was close. During the summer the two girls, both of whom
had grown up in the upper middle class, promised one another
that they would never buy a sofa or chair made with natural
fibers. A year after college both enrolled in the master's program
in social work at Bryn Mawr College as their first step toward
careers in social work and in the nonprofit sector.

These friends were my first face-to-face confrontation with
the problem of good—the puzzle of why those who reject Christianity often seem better, and contribute more, than Christians
do. I had become convinced of the truth of Christianity at about
the same time that my friends were giving up natural fibers. The
problem of evil did not trouble me a great deal then. The
origins of evil might be a mystery, but its pervasiveness certainly
was not. As I looked at myself and the world around me, the

Bible's claims that each of us is sinful and that human social and political structures are tainted by sin seemed indisputably true.

The problem of good was far more troubling. My friends did not have any particular interest in Christianity, but each had a passionate desire to "visit orphans and widows in their affliction," as the epistle of James puts it (James 1:27). They were committed to meeting the needs of those around them, and in neither case has this passion dimmed. Although I concocted reasons to the contrary, by any plausible yardstick my friends were much better people than I was, and I cannot claim to have surpassed or even equaled them since.

The puzzle has two different sides. The dark side is the behavior of us who call ourselves Christians. Why, as C. S. Lewis put it, can bad or disagreeable people still be found in our churches? And why have Christians been responsible for so many atrocities throughout the course of history? These are important questions, and they have generated a great deal of thoughtful discussion, particularly in recent years. Lewis pointed out, for example, that it would be misleading simply to compare the goodness or badness of a Christian to that of a non-Christian, even if we could perfectly assess their relative goodness. The more relevant question is whether a Christian has improved since embracing Christianity, not what kind of person she was when she first came to church.[1] Jesus himself said that the sick are the ones who most need a doctor, not those who are well. Defenders of Christianity acknowledge that Christians have been involved in awful misbehavior, from the Crusades to Christian defenses of slavery, but they point out that these actions are a perversion of Christ's teachings and that Christianity has produced a great deal of good when the church has hewed to teachings of her Lord.

Although the badness of Christians is a tremendously important issue, this chapter will be much more concerned with the other side of the problem of good: the awesome good that some non-Christians do. As anyone who has read this far into this book will recognize, the traditional term for this side of the problem of good, at least for those of us who trace our theological lineage back to the Protestant Reformation, is common grace. John Calvin seems to have been the first to articulate the doctrine in something like its modern form. Marveling at the wisdom of the ancient philosophers and at other examples of goodness in those who have not placed their faith in Jesus Christ, Calvin concluded that "those virtues are not the common properties of nature, but the peculiar graces of God, which he dispenses in great variety, and in a certain degree to men that are otherwise profane."[2] Although Calvin himself emphasized that the virtues were *not* common—since they reflect God's intervention in the world—subsequent theologians such as Abraham Kuyper have called God's grace in these areas "common" to distinguish it from the saving, or "special," grace experienced by those who have committed themselves to Christ.

Perhaps because I am a legal scholar, three issues come immediately to my mind when I think about the practical implications of common grace for our involvement in, and reflection on, the world. The first is charitable giving to non-Christian organizations. When we are solicited by the Red Cross or the college we attended, should we immediately throw the letter away, or might there be a role for Christian contributions to non-Christian organizations? Second is politics. How should Christians think about voting and about their role in secular politics? The final issue is broader questions of justice. What might the doctrine of common grace tell us about the proper ends of justice and about the relationship between Christian and non-Christian justice initiatives?

Although these questions of charity, politics, and justice are my principal focus, this chapter begins with a few additional comments about common grace, and it concludes in a more speculative mode by considering whether the good done by non-Christians like my two friends has any eternal significance if they never become Christians.

Wrestling with Common Grace

John Murray begins his well-known treatment of common grace by posing the same question my friends modeled for me:

> How is it that men [and women] who are not savingly renewed by the Spirit of God nevertheless exhibit so many qualities, gifts and accomplishments that promote the preservation, temporal happiness, cultural progress, social and economic improvement of themselves and of others? How is it that races and peoples that have been apparently untouched by the redemptive and regenerative influences of the gospel contribute so much to what we call human civilization?[3]

Part of the answer, in Murray's view, is that God restrains the evil that might otherwise overwhelm the possibility of human flourishing. But Murray, like his predecessors, also insists that common grace has a positive dimension. God "not only restrains evil in men," he says, "but he also endows men with gifts, talents, and aptitudes; he stimulates them with interest and purpose to the practice of virtues, the pursuance of worthy tasks, and the cultivation of arts and sciences that . . . make for the benefit and civilization of the human race."[4]

Christians do not have a great deal of difficulty appreciating the virtues of those who have come long before us. Indeed, some seem so virtuous—so "Christian" in their outlook—that we are tempted to speculate that perhaps they experienced God's saving grace even if they would not have recognized this themselves. Augustine so admired Plato that he imagined that Plato might have been a Christian had he lived in the Christian era. Dante adopted the Roman poet Virgil as his guide in

The Inferno. And though Dante could not quite imagine the pagan poet in paradise, he envisioned a pleasant eternity for him rather than the torments of hell.

Acknowledging common grace in the present sometimes seems harder, and as a result it can pose different problems. This is not due to a lack of biblical models. Perhaps the best-known biblical teaching comes in Jeremiah 29, which records Jeremiah's prophetic instructions as Israel was being overrun and much of its population deported to Babylon. Jeremiah tells the exiles that God expects them to build houses and plant gardens, and more generally to "seek the welfare of the city where [he has] sent you into exile, and pray to the LORD on its behalf, for in its welfare you will find your welfare" (Jer. 29:7). The book of Daniel offers an object lesson on what it looks like to honor this instruction, as do Esther's involvement in the royal court of Persia and Joseph's much earlier career in Egypt.

In recent years Christian leaders have offered radically different visions for cultural engagement. According to one strand of recent Christian thinking, America was once a Christian nation—a conclusion that implies that it might be possible to restore this status. This perspective suggests that Christians should engage the culture with the intent of transforming it. Other Christians have advocated a very different stance. In response to the controversy generated by evangelical involvement in political and social issues, they have advocated that Christians bring a halt to their involvement in these issues, at least for a period of time.

As different as they are, the two stances have one very important quality in common: both seem to deny the existence of common grace. The call to re-Christianize American society implies that there is nothing valuable in our current social and political institutions. They should simply be bulldozed and new Christian structures erected in their place. Advocates of a Christian "time-out" do not take an explicit stand on the merits or demerits of current culture. But their stance suggests that the culture is irrelevant for Christians, at least for the time being.

What does it mean to engage the culture but not to assume that this engagement will produce a pervasively Christian culture? One way to answer this question is to consider the implications of God's sovereignty over the unfolding of human history, as a few of the best-known theologians of common grace have done. But I think it may also be helpful to get down to particulars and to wrestle with a few of the contexts in which questions of common grace arise.

Charitable Giving

We all confront questions of common grace when we decide how to donate money each year. Although the Bible does not say how much we should give to our church, most Christians come to roughly the same conclusions about these issues, even if in practice our words and dollars do not always end up in the same place. The former pastor of the church I attend used to say that, since the Israelites were commanded to give ten percent of their income in the Old Testament, we surely should give at least this much now, considering the abundance of God's blessings to us in the new covenant. Most Christians would agree that ten percent of our gross income should be the baseline as we think about our yearly giving.

But what about giving to non-Christian organizations? A few Christians question whether it is ever appropriate to donate money to non-Christian organizations, given our primary obligation to the body of Christ. Most would not take so unyielding a stance, but most Christians I know give only tepidly to non-Christian organizations—in amounts that are trivial in comparison to their Christian giving. I suspect this is due to doubts about whether we should make substantial investments in organizations that are not committed to the gospel.

If God truly does work through the lives of non-Christians as well as Christians, as the theology of common grace suggests, perhaps we need to revisit these attitudes toward non-Christian organizations. Many of us may be called to give generously to non-Christian efforts. Perhaps surprisingly, those who believe that the government is too involved in the provision of social services, and that its role should be more limited, may be particularly called to give generously to non-Christian activities. If private organizations are to fill the gap, they obviously need considerable private funding. Notice, in this regard, how Old Testament tithes were used. Some of the funds were used to support priests and Levites as well as the sacrificial system, but the tithes also helped to finance functions that we would now describe as civil government.

In my view, the key question is not whether Christians should invest their time and money in non-Christian charities—surely we should—but how Christians should approach this involvement. Two recent trends in charitable giving seem especially noteworthy in this regard. The first is the proliferation of "naming opportunities"—the practice of luring donors by promising to name a building or other item in honor of the man or woman who financed it. Should Christians resist the naming phenomenon, embrace it, or take some other stance? I suspect that most Christians would call for resistance for very good biblical reasons. Inviting an organization to name a building in our honor bears an uncomfortable resemblance to Saul's decision to have an altar erected in his honor after defeating the Amalekites, to the love of self that led to the fall, and to the idolatry that the prophets and Jesus all inveighed against. These are important concerns, but I do not think we can say that Christian donors should never accept the honor of being recognized for their charity. A donor's willingness to be named may be courageous in some cases, or may vividly demonstrate Christians' care for "the welfare of the city." Most of us do not object when we are included on a list of donors to an art museum or orchestra, and I do not think we are invariably wrong to allow this. Perhaps the best starting point is to seriously consider the risk that pride is our real motivation before agreeing to forego anonymity.

The other dramatic recent trend in charitable giving is the effort to monitor the performance of nonprofit organizations more carefully and to run them more like ordinary businesses. Bill Gates is perhaps the best-known example of a philanthropist bringing carefully calibrated business plans to the nonprofit world in the projects he finances for the Gates Foundation. Other major donors, such as the founders of Google, are equally focused on outcomes, results, and the achievement of excellence. From the perspective of the beneficiaries of services provided by nonprofit organizations—whether it be quality schooling in the United States or mosquito nets in Africa—the increased attention to efficiency carries obvious benefits. From the donors' perspective, on the other hand, the implications are more equivocal. The new model invites the donor to believe that he or she is in control at every step of the process, and the insistence on control can itself be a way to exalt ourselves. There is something to be said for relinquishing control—as, of course, our Lord did—rather than demanding an identifiable return for the dollars or time we contribute.[5]

The Political Sphere

A second set of issues arises from our involvement in the political sphere. With the possible exception of the strictest Anabaptists, each of us is involved in politics at some level. And even those who distance themselves from the political fray are taking a political stance, as Stanley Hauerwas has long pointed out.[6] Our immersion in politics intersects with common grace at three points.

For those of us who live in a democracy, the one unavoidable question is whether we should vote. During the American presidential elections of the 2000s, a handful of prominent American evangelicals announced that they did not intend to vote for either candidate. Their reasoning was in some respects

94

quite compelling: the platforms of both major candidates deviated in serious respects from biblical teaching, with the Democrats endorsing abortion and the Republicans proposing to ratchet back government protection of the poor. Although we cannot rule out the possibility of an election that is so corrupt that Christians should refuse to vote, the biblical teachings on common grace would seem to counsel in favor of voting under all but the most extreme circumstances. Christians' frustration with the parties' deviations from biblical teaching was understandable, but participating in an election is one small way we contribute to the good of the society in which we find ourselves.

A few Christians are far more intimately involved in the political process as candidates, staffers, or those who wield influence with candidates or staffers. I have already mentioned the recent suggestions that Christians should avoid these entanglements for a time. As with the decision to forgo voting, it is not easy to reconcile such calls with the Bible's teachings on common grace. Christians would probably be wise to do more showing—that is, to focus more on the example we set in how we live our lives—and less telling, but abandoning politics would be an odd way to seek the welfare of the city.

In countries with parliamentary systems of government, Christians can take this form of direct involvement even further by forming a Christian political party. In late nineteenth-century Holland, Abraham Kuyper did just this. His Anti-Revolution party assailed the legacy of the French Revolution and advocated Reformed Christian principles. There are obvious benefits to this strategy. In the United States evangelical Christians have been closely identified with a single secular political party for the past generation. This identification can create the appearance of hypocrisy when the party's commitments seem to depart from biblical values. Starting an explicitly Christian political party, much as Christians have founded Christian schools and universities, might enable Christians to align their religious and political commitments more closely.

Christian political parties may also more naturally reflect the Bible's teachings on common grace than Christian schools do. Unlike Christian schools, which can insulate Christians from their secular neighbors, politics requires direct engagement with those with whom we disagree.

This strategy also carries serious downsides, however. The most obvious is that there is no single, clearly correct biblical answer for many political issues. Christians can and do reach different conclusions about the best immigration policy or about strategies for addressing poverty. To suggest that one party's answer to these questions is the only Christian answer is to treat as principial—that is, as a central truth of our faith—even those issues on which discretion is inevitable and cannot be avoided. This does not mean that Christian political parties are invariably misguided. But Christian political parties do not solve the dilemmas of political engagement; they substitute one set of challenges for another.

Justice and Human Rights

The law school where I teach, like many law schools, offers several different classes concerning the law of human rights. These classes are extremely popular, and more than a few of the students who enroll in them have come to law school with a vision for spending their careers promoting and defending human rights. In many of these classes Christianity is never mentioned. Most of the students are not themselves Christians, and they might not see international human rights as having anything to do with Christianity. Yet many human rights initiatives, such as efforts to protect victims of genocide and to prosecute its perpetrators, seem to promote justice. They are organizations and initiatives peopled by non-Christians like my two college friends. What does common grace tell us about these quests for justice?

If God is at work throughout the world, as common grace assures us that he is, we can expect to see evidence of biblical values even in secular human rights initiatives. And we do. When advocates protest genocide or call for better treatment of women in developing countries, they frequently draw on notions of dignity that borrow from the biblical teaching that each of us is made in the image of God, even if the advocates themselves do not recognize the connection. The European framework for justice is based on principles of subsidiarity—the idea that issues should be devolved to the level of government that can handle them most effectively—that have deep roots in Catholic Social Thought and in Abraham Kuyper's closely analogous concept of sphere sovereignty. Yet recent history also suggests that it is possible to contribute to justice without acknowledging or appealing to God. We see this secular orientation in theory as well as in practice. Some of the most influential advocates of human rights, like the economist and philosopher Amartya Sen, steer clear of religion; others—the ethicist Peter Singer is the leading example—self-consciously erect their appeals on non-theistic foundations.[7]

One obvious response to the secularization of human rights discourse is to identify the points at which secular human rights theory diverges from biblical teaching and why these departures matter. Singer and other secular human rights theorists some-times highlight human "agency"—our ability to make decisions and develop a plan for our lives—as the basis of human dignity. This conception suggests that those who lack these capacities, such as babies and the mentally impaired, are not entitled to the same respect as those whose mental capacities are mature and unimpaired. The Bible, by contrast, teaches that every human is made in the image of God and fully loved by God, regard-less of his or her capacities. These distinctions have profound implications for issues like abortion and euthanasia. Christians are right to insist on a biblical vision of dignity and to challenge the secular alternatives.

But Christians can also learn from secular teaching on human rights, much as Augustine and Calvin learned from the insights of the classical pagan philosophers. Sen has developed a model for human rights that he refers to as a "capabilities" approach. Rather than measuring progress in the developing world solely in monetary terms such as gross domestic product, Sen argues for an emphasis on educational opportunities, access to health care, and other factors that determine whether a person can fully participate in the society. In my view these insights would fit quite neatly within a more fully developed Christian vision of human rights.[8]

A Philadelphia lawyer named William Clark has recently developed an alternative to traditional corporations in a somewhat similar spirit. Inspired in part by secular efforts to promote social responsibility, Clark has drawn up a blueprint for an entity he calls a "benefit corporation."[9] Although they resemble ordinary corporations in most respects, benefit corporations are required to identify their social objectives—such as community building or care for the environment—and to conduct a yearly audit to assess how well the business has honored these commitments. Although there is nothing explicitly Christian about a benefit corporation, Clark has modeled the framework on biblical values such as our obligations to love our neighbors and to care for the creation. Fourteen states have passed legislation permitting businesses to identify themselves as benefit corporations.

An inevitable question is whether the church has a role to play in these human rights or justice initiatives. The greatest American exemplar of social justice in the twentieth century, the Civil Rights Movement, was grounded directly in black churches. More recently, some evangelical churches have worked directly with International Justice Mission, an organization that comes to the aid of victims of sexual trafficking and other forms of slavery, often by prodding local authorities to enforce laws that are already on the books.

The principal concern when churches participate directly in these activities is that the involvement will distract them from their responsibility to make disciples and nurture the body of Christ—that the church will cease to be the church. This concern was far less an issue for the black church in the Civil Rights Movement era because the same discrimination that the movement sought to end assured that the church would not simply merge into the society around it. But there have been costs even for black churches, and the risks of direct involvement in justice initiatives for other churches are much greater, as some mainline Protestant denominations have discovered.

Perhaps the best model for most churches is to serve as an incubator for human rights and justice. Churches have a central role in forming Christians' understanding of biblical teaching on these issues, just as they do in other areas. At the least this will mean that biblical values shape interactions within the church and influence more generally how church members understand the issues.

In some cases this may lead to the birth of a new ministry. The church I attend sometimes sponsors these ministries in their early stages, with the understanding that they will spin off to become separate from the church. This model—which has been used with a crisis pregnancy center, an AIDS ministry, and a ministry concerned with sexual issues—strikes me as an effective strategy for maintaining a church's focus on salvation and discipleship without turning its back on the domain of common grace.

Does Common Grace Have Eternal Value?

I haven't forgotten about my friends, and I would like to conclude this brief chapter by considering a question I may not have the answer to: assuming that my friends and others like them do not ever accept the free gift offered by Christ, will any of their work have eternal significance, or will it be consumed in the final judgment?

The Bible does not give a clear answer to this question, but it does provide a few clues. The first comes in the passages that speak about the eternal future of the heavens and earth. Although Christians have sometimes imagined that the earth will one day explode and disappear, the Bible actually tells of transformation, not destruction. The creation groans in travail, as the apostle Paul puts it, looking forward to this day of transformation (Rom. 8:20–23). The closing chapters of Revelation show the New Jerusalem descending to earth (Rev. 21:1–4). Nor will those who inhabit the New Jerusalem be disembodied souls. Our resurrection will, in some mysterious way, be physical, which is why we attest to the "resurrection of the body" when we say the Apostles' Creed.

The other set of clues concerns the works done by those of us who claim Christ as our Savior. Although the Bible repeatedly affirms that salvation comes through faith, not works, the New Testament subtly but insistently teaches that our works will also be subject to scrutiny. Jesus suggests that the rewards of heaven will be especially great for those who have tended to the needs of their brothers and sisters. Paul describes a testing by fire, in which some of his and other preachers' work will, like gold or silver, survive while other work will be burned up like straw (1 Cor. 3:13–15). He later warns that "we must all appear before the judgment seat of Christ, so that each one may receive what is due for what he has done in the body, whether good or evil" (2 Cor. 5:10).

As we weigh these clues we might plausibly conclude that the only works that will stand in the judgment are the contributions of those who are in Christ. Much as one worker in the field will be saved while others will be left behind, the transformed creation may perfect the work done by Christians to foster justice and beauty. In this view the noblest contributions of non-Christians are burned up like chaff.

But the clues can also be interpreted to suggest that the contributions to justice of non-Christians such as my two friends may also have eternal significance. Richard Mouw is perhaps the best-known recent advocate of something like this second possibility. Mouw notes, in this regard, an intriguing shift in Isaiah's prophecies. In Isaiah's great picture of Israel's future glory in chapter 60, he describes the same ships of Tarshish that were earlier slated for destruction as carrying God's people into the Promised Land, and as evidence of worldwide hope for the Lord. The "artifacts of Tarshish" will thus be in the Holy City, along with the work of God's people, now seen in eternal perspective.[10]

This does not mean that the builders of Tarshish will be saved even if they never turned to God, of course. The suggestion that non-Christians' contributions to justice and beauty may have eternal significance must be considered together with the Bible's teaching that even our most impressive-seeming works cannot save us—they are as filthy rags, as Isaiah 64:6 (KJV) so pungently puts it. Together they hint that the work of non-Christians may contribute to God's transformation of the heavens and earth, even as the non-Christians themselves will be forsaken for having rejected Christ.

The possibility that the finest artifacts of common grace will endure may seem at first to dilute the significance of special grace. It might even seem to suggest, as Marion Clark points out in this book's introduction, that special grace is unnecessary. But quite the contrary is true, or so it seems to me. To contribute to justice and beauty and then to be banished from enjoying its fulfillment would be the most excruciating of agonies. In the most literal sense, the exclusion would be hell. Yet all who turn to Christ and reconcile themselves to God through him will participate in the new heavens and new earth. The radical contrast intensifies both common and special grace. Common grace contributes directly to the ultimate transformation, yet even those who contribute the most exquisite beauty or profound justice will be lost apart from Christ.

Although I am persuaded that some of the wonders of common grace may have eternal significance, I am neither a theologian nor the son of a theologian, and the last several paragraphs should be taken in that light. But the principal questions with which this chapter has been concerned are far less esoteric. If we take the Bible's teachings about common grace to heart, they will shape our thinking about practical issues such as donations to charities, involvement in issues of justice, and participation in politics. In this short chapter I have attempted to offer thoughts and raise questions about what this might look like as we seek to honor our Lord in the world.

For Discussion

1. Do you agree with the author that you should contribute effort and money to secular causes? How should a Christian divide time and money between Christian and secular causes?

2. Are there situations in which it is best for a Christian not to vote or be involved in political issues?

3. Should there be specifically Christian political parties or movements?

4. Is there a distinction between churches' being involved in political processes and individual Christians' being involved?

5. Do you agree with the author that secularists can produce right thinking on matters of justice? Where does he see distinctions between secularists and biblical thinking on justice issues?

6. How involved do you think churches should be in addressing justice issues?

7. Is it necessary for a church, Christian ministry, or individual to transform a culture in order for their involvement to be meaningful?

8. Do you agree with the author that Scripture suggests that the work of non-Christians may endure and even contribute to God's transformation of the heavens and earth to come?

How May We Learn from the World?

Gene Edward Veith

"LET EVERY GOOD and true Christian understand that wherever truth may be found, it belongs to his Master."[1] So said Augustine in *On Christian Doctrine* (2.18.28)—apparently the source of the slogan "All truth is God's truth."

It seems self-evident that if an idea, discovery, or insight is true, even though it comes from a non-Christian, it must also accord with Christian truth. This means that Christians may access all knowledge from all sources, freely drawing on insights from literature, science, education, philosophy, the arts, and other fields, no matter how secular or worldly the source may seem. And yet it is also evident that the world is a place of sin, rebellion, and false worldviews. How can a Christian learn, in any significant way, from someone whose very presuppositions, modes of thinking, and views of the world are opposed to God's revelation because of sin?

The above quotation from Augustine continues, "and while he recognizes and acknowledges the truth, even in [pagan] religious literature, let him reject the figments of superstition."[2] The sentence comes in the context of Augustine's searing critique of pagan and classical learning. He is wrestling over what elements of pagan or, rather, classical Greek and

Roman learning Christians may appropriate, and while he finds factual material and skills such as logic and rhetoric helpful, he rejects more than he accepts. Augustine is not giving Christians a blank check to accept anything and everything that seems to be of value in the world. His criterion is "truth," and he describes a process of sifting and winnowing to eliminate the "figments of superstition" that underlie much of "worldly" learning.

In this chapter I hope to provide a framework for showing why and how we may learn from the world while always staying grounded on the Word of God.

Paul and Epimenides

When the apostle Paul was in Athens, "his spirit was provoked within him" at the rampant idolatry (Acts 17:16). He debated not only those who followed false religions but also the Epicurean and Stoic philosophers (v. 18). In his sermon at the Areopagus—the hill of Ares, god of war, where a court met that regulated the religious life of Athens—Paul dismantled the foundations of the pagan religion and yet, at the same time, borrowed from it to make his case.

Not only does he affirm and proclaim the "unknown God" to whom an altar had been dedicated, he approvingly quotes from both kinds of his adversaries, a pagan and a philosopher (v. 28): "In him we live and move and have our being." This comes from Epimenides of Crete in a hymn to Zeus. "For we are indeed his offspring" comes from Aratus the Stoic.[3]

Epimenides was a poet of legendary proportions for the Greeks, but only fragments of a few of his writings have survived through quotations from other authors. In 1912 the great Bible scholar J. Rendel Harris pieced together the original text, a passage from a poem entitled *Minos* of over one thousand lines:

> The Cretans have fashioned a tomb for thee, O Holy and High!
> Liars, evil beasts, idle bellies;

For thou diest not: forever thou livest and standest;
For in thee we live and move and have our being.[4]

So Epimenides is also the source of the "lying Cretans" quotation in Titus 1:12—in fact, it comes from the same passage, just before the line that he quotes in the Areopagus! The reason the Cretans were considered liars, as Harris shows, is that they actually claimed that a certain structure in Crete was the tomb of Zeus. This infuriated pious Greeks, though later Christian apologists like Lactantius would jump on the story to make the case that Zeus was originally just a man.[5] Epimenides is saying that his fellow Cretans are "liars" for making that claim and for bringing the deity down to the level of a mortal man. This is at least parallel to Paul's insisting to the Athenians that the "divine being" is not "an image formed by the art and imagination of man" (Acts 17:29).

But Epimenides thought that we live and move and have our being in Zeus. Paul in his sermon is repudiating the entire Greek pantheon, whose altars were lined up single file in the marketplace. He recognizes that this line from the pagan hymn shows a larger conception of deity than that of the superhuman Zeus of the myths and graven images. Paul, not being constrained by the author's original intention, sees in the poem an intimation of the "unknown God" already being postulated by Greek philosophers, who also rejected the myths and the gods made by hand. Plato, Aristotle, and Stoics like Aratus realized that the creation testifies to a Creator—the aspect of God that Paul emphasizes—but their problem is that this transcendent deity is "unknown." Their intellect took them in the right direction but could only take them so far before they ran into a dead end. They knew that there was a god, but they could not know God. For that they needed God's own revelation of himself. So Paul, inspired by the Holy Spirit, gave them God's Word: "What therefore you worship as unknown, this I proclaim to you" (v. 23).

Paul is involved with the world he is evangelizing. He is not separating himself from it. He is interacting with pagans and secularists. He reads their literature and even knows some of it by memory. He is not, however, accepting it uncritically, much less revising his theology according to the fashions of the world. But he is finding truth, goodness, and beauty among the work of nonbelievers and claiming it for Christ.

In Him We Live and Move and Have Our Being

The reason he is able to do so, of course, is given in the very passage from Epimenides that he is quoting. "In him we live and move and have our being" (Acts 17:28). God providentially governs everything, including the lives and being of the pagan Athenians to whom Paul is preaching. This is by virtue of his creation of all things. "God," says Paul, "made the world and everything in it," which makes him "Lord of heaven and earth" (v. 24).

We often think of creation as what occurred at some time in the past. That is only one aspect of God's creative work. "And God *said*, 'Let there be . . .'" and light, the heavens, the earth, living things, and human beings all came into existence (Gen. 1:3–26). God spoke them into being; that is, he created by means of his word. "By the word of the LORD the heavens were made" (Ps. 33:6). The Bible also teaches that God at every moment continues to keep his creation in existence. Again, he does so by speaking, by his word. God—specifically God the Son—"upholds the universe by the word of his power" (Heb. 1:3).

John makes the connection between the word of God, the creation, and the second person of the Trinity, who became flesh as Jesus Christ.

> In the beginning was the Word, and the Word was with God, and the Word was God. He was in the beginning with God. All things were made through him, and without him was not any thing made that was made. . . .

106

And the Word became flesh and dwelt among us, and we have seen his glory, glory as of the only Son from the Father, full of grace and truth. (John 1:1–3, 14)

In a remarkable passage in Colossians, Paul says that not only were all things *made* by Christ, they are also *sustained* by Christ and exist *for* Christ.

For by him all things were created, in heaven and on earth, visible and invisible, whether thrones or dominions or rulers or authorities—all things were created through him and for him. And he is before all things, and in him all things hold together. And he is the head of the body, the church. He is the beginning, the firstborn from the dead, that in everything he might be preeminent. For in him all the fullness of God was pleased to dwell, and through him to reconcile to himself all things, whether on earth or in heaven, making peace by the blood of his cross. (Col. 1:16–20)

To use Aristotelian terms that would have been familiar to the Athenians, Christ is both the First Cause (the origin) and the Final Cause (the end, the purpose). He is "the Alpha and the Omega, the first and the last, the beginning and the end" (Rev. 22:13). An object is what it is not only because of the way it was made but also because of its future purpose. The *logos* (the Word) is also the *telos* (the purpose), which accounts for the design of everything in creation. And this *logos* of Greek philosophy is the Word of God, who "became flesh and dwelt among us."

In his relationship to his creation Christ is the beginning and the end, and he is the present as well. "In him all things hold together." As the King James Version puts it, "by him all things consist." Christ is described as the originator of everything in existence, the glue that holds together everything that exists, and the one for whom everything exists.

But surely sin and the fall damaged this close relationship between Christ and "all things"? Indeed, but the passage

107

from Colossians speaks of this intimacy in terms of not only creation but also redemption. "In him all the fullness of God was pleased to dwell, and through him to reconcile to himself all things, whether on earth or in heaven, making peace by the blood of his cross." To "reconcile" means to bring into unity things that are opposed. Christ's atonement redeems sinners, to be sure, and also "all things." Christ's victory is complete. He is "preeminent" in "everything."

These passages continually refer to the scope of Christ's lordship extending to "all things" and "everything." Such language leaves nothing out. "Everything" would include Epimenides and his poem to Zeus. Christ made Epimenides and gave him his talent. He sustains Epimenides and holds together his body and the language, logic, and aesthetic principles that make his poem possible. Epimenides and his poem exist for Christ.

Thus, creation, providence, redemption, and the preeminence of Christ mean that "all things" are encompassed in his lordship. This means that "all things" are, in principle, the domain of Christ's people. As 1 Corinthians 3:21–23 says,

> For all things are yours, whether Paul or Apollos or Cephas or the world or life or death or the present or the future—all are yours, and you are Christ's, and Christ is God's.

If There Is Any Excellence, If There Is Anything Worthy of Praise

We must not, of course, neglect or underestimate the effect of sin in the world. In the new heaven and the new earth that await us Christians' relationship with the creation will find its fulfillment, restoring the conditions of the paradise that God intended but that has been lost. Now it may be that " 'all things are lawful,' but not all things are helpful. 'All things are lawful,' but not all things build up" (1 Cor. 10:23). Sin infects those in the world, distorting what we might otherwise learn from nonbelievers. The epistemological implications of sin mean that unbelievers are limited in their ability to apprehend truth, and they also mean that believers have great difficulty in discerning, with their own powers, what is true and false.

The world is Christ's, to be sure, but we are warned against being "worldly." The Devil claims to be the prince of this world, presumptuously offering "all the kingdoms of the world and their glory" to Jesus as his gift (Matt. 4:8), saying, "To you I will give all this authority and their glory, for it has been delivered to me, and I give it to whom I will" (Luke 4:6). Satan must have missed the irony that he was making this offer to the King of Kings. Satan is a usurper, and he wreaks havoc in the world. But the Devil, who is concerned mostly with the spiritual realm, does not have sovereignty over God's creation. Nevertheless, we dare not minimize the dangers of sin and the Devil.

> And you were dead in the trespasses and sins in which you once walked, following the course of this world, following the prince of the power of the air, the spirit that is now at work in the sons of disobedience—among whom we all once lived in the passions of our flesh, carrying out the desires of the body and the mind, and were by nature children of wrath, like the rest of mankind. (Eph. 2:1–3)

We must no longer be engaged in "following the course of this world." The desires of the body lead us astray, and so do the desires of the mind. The world may belong to God, but how and to what extent can we learn from the world of unbelievers without being deceived, either by the Devil or by our own minds?

God creates and sustains by his Word, his Word who is the Son of God became flesh to reconcile us and all things to himself, and he gives us his Word in the pages of Scripture. So the Bible can help us to discern what is from God—including things we might learn from the world—and what is not.

The Bible's teaching about sin makes clear that Gentiles— that is, those who do not believe in the God of Abraham—

know the moral law, even though they know nothing of God's revelation.

> For when Gentiles, who do not have the law, by nature do what the law requires, they are a law to themselves, even though they do not have the law. They show that the work of the law is written on their hearts, while their conscience also bears witness, and their conflicting thoughts accuse or even excuse them. (Rom. 2:14–15)

Now "nature" in this sense does not mean trees and wildlife and unspoiled wilderness. It is more like what we express in phrases such as "the nature of things" or "human nature." That is, "nature" refers to objective reality, to God's creation. Whatever or whoever partakes of the reality that God has created will be in accord with him. Most of our problems come from our sinful, subjective selves and from expressing our sinfulness in the world. This text says that even unbelievers who know nothing of God's revelation through his Word in some sense can know and even to a certain extent "do what the law requires" "by nature."

By virtue of God's creation they are humans living in the actual world; as such, "human nature" demands that they will have to cooperate with other members of society. They are also, as the Ephesians passage we have quoted above reminds us, "by nature children of wrath" (2:3). Their fallen "nature" is such that they are sinful and depraved. But the way the universe is made ensures that these Gentiles behave, at least on the surface, with a measure of self-control. Those who indulge their sinful nature by stealing, murdering, and otherwise harming their neighbors will face the consequences, as pagans know quite well how to execute justice.

The law "written on their hearts" leaves them without excuse for their sins and exposes them to the just wrath of God. "By nature" they have a conscience. This creates "conflicting thoughts" between their sinful impulses and what they know, deep down, is right. Their conflicts of conscience "accuse" them. But they can also "excuse" them. Nonbelievers sometimes do follow their consciences.

Thus, a nonbeliever might be a source of moral education. The early church often held up pagan writers as offering powerful moral examples. In Homer's *Odyssey*, for instance, the hero's adventures involve him in moral trials, which have been instructive for readers then and now. The Sirens depict the dangerous deceptions of temptation; the lotus-eaters demonstrate why it is not a good idea to take drugs; the Cyclops shows how anarchy begets stupidity; Circe turning humans into pigs shows the necessity of restraining one's appetite; the reunion of Odysseus with his family shows the obligation of a man to protect his household, to be faithful to his wife, and to nurture his son. To be sure, Odysseus often fails morally, as when he succumbs to the seduction of Calypso and when he abandons his family to seek glory by fighting the Trojan War. But those failures, no less than the positive examples, also teach morality when we see their tragic consequences.

Nonbelievers might be able to teach us something about morality. Their knowledge will be imperfect, lacking the clarity of God's Word, but a "gentile" might still inspire us toward good behavior. Ancient Greek literature praises virtues—particularly the so-called "natural virtues" of justice, prudence, temperance, and fortitude—but it has virtually nothing to say about the "theological virtues" of faith, hope, and love. We might get "law" from a gentile. But we cannot get "gospel." Christianity does not give us a new moral law, just the same moral law that is universal to human nature, and which all people both admire and violate. Christianity is all about how to find forgiveness for violating that morality. It requires the Word of God that the Holy Spirit uses to convict us of our sin and convey the grace of Christ.

Because the created order is God's domain and individuals are sinners, we should focus mostly on objective meaning rather than on expressive meaning. That is, a nonbeliever may convey something that is objectively true and valuable despite himself. Again, Epimenides said something worthy of being included in Holy Scripture, even though he himself intended it to refer to Zeus. But Paul recognized that what he said—"In him we live and move and have our being"—applied rather to the true God. It is not the author's intention that matters so much as what the author said. A non-Christian author can express Christian truth. There is hardly a more moving presentation of Christian grace in all literature (or drama, or movies) than in the redemption of Valjean in *Les Misérables*. But was Victor Hugo, the author, a Christian? Probably not in the way most of us would recognize. But in the course of telling a powerful story he expressed Christian truth.

The very "nature" of a work of art can partake of God's created order and thus be "good" despite its unbelieving author or maker. Augustine believed that form comes from God as part of his creation.[6] Thus mathematics, logic, the laws of nature and of aesthetics, as well as other ordering principles are part of the *logos*—God's design that underlies all things. A painting made by an unbeliever and expressing a false worldview may still display mastery of form in its orchestration of color, its composition, and its technical mastery. Thus a Christian might critique its theme and its implicit worldview while still appreciating its beauty. In literary art a poet might not know Christ, but his language is a gift of God, as are the laws of harmonics for a musician.

By its nature, fiction, whether in a novel or in a film, involves the interaction of plot and character. A plot must involve some sort of conflict. More often than not, that conflict will be a moral one, whether on the simplest level between "good guys" and "bad guys" or in the inner struggles of a complicated character. This holds true even if the author is a notorious sinner. In some cases today authors might consciously turn traditional conventions upside down, turning the villain (say, a criminal) into an "anti-hero" in conflict with an upright member of society (say, a policeman). Moral issues still insinuate themselves, with the criminal being given good qualities (such as sensitivity to justice) and the policeman being portrayed as corrupt.

The fact is, it is very difficult to make a character sympathetic to the audience without some moral appeal. Thus, work with no moral value whatsoever (pornography, hate literature, exploitation films) is typically bad not only morally but also aesthetically. Surprisingly often, the conflict between good and evil is resolved when one character sacrifices himself for another.

The best guidelines are given in Scripture. "Whatever is true, whatever is honorable, whatever is just, whatever is pure, whatever is lovely, whatever is commendable, if there is any excellence, if there is anything worthy of praise, think about these things" (Phil. 4:8). The operative word here is "whatever." This is not the "whatever" of the bored, apathetic relativist. It's the "whatever" of God's comprehensive, all-encompassing creation. The criteria is not whether the source is a Christian, it is the nature of the work. Non-Christian artists may produce work that is "lovely," that has "excellence," that is "worthy of praise." Non-Christian thinkers can articulate ideas that are "true," "honorable," "just," and "pure." The King James Version renders the word for "commendable" as "of good report"—that is, having a good reputation. Books and other works that have a good reputation—classics, works that have entered the secular "canon," critically acclaimed achievements—may have a claim on the Christian's attention.

Many Christians today have the habit of attending only to the "content" of a work—approving it if it has a Christian message, even if its aesthetic quality is dreadful, and rejecting it if it expresses a worldview that is not Christian, even if its aesthetic quality is excellent. An Augustinian approach favors works of the highest quality, *whatever* the source may be. While recognizing that form and content are intrinsically connected, if not inseparable, an Augustinian can interact with and possibly reject the ideas of a work, whether articulated by a non-Christian or a Christian, while still glorifying God for "whatever" in the work is "worthy of praise."

Walking through Today's Areopagus

Christians speak much today about "winning the world for Christ," "advancing the kingdom of God," and "transforming the culture." To be sure, the society in which we find ourselves has drifted far from God's will, and Christians should do what they can to battle the evils of the day. And yet Christians must keep in mind that, in another sense, the world is *already* Christ's, that God *already* rules as the King over all things, and that God *continues to work* even in apparently godless cultures.

God reigns over and actively governs both his spiritual kingdom and the universe that he has created, including human societies. He rules his creation through his providence and his laws (the moral law for human beings, the natural laws for the physical realm). An important means that he uses to care for and provide for his creation is the various vocations to which he calls human beings (1 Cor. 7:17).

Luther, the great theologian of vocation, emphasized that our various callings are not simply matters of what we must do; in addition, God himself works through human vocations.[7] God gives us our daily bread by means of farmers, millers, and bakers. He creates new life by means of fathers and mothers. He protects us by means of magistrates and the legal system. Luther goes so far as to say that God is "hidden" in vocation, that he milks the cows through the hands of the milkmaid just as he proclaims his Word through the mouths of pastors. Though God can work miraculously, without means, he prefers to give his gifts through human beings. As the source of every good and perfect gift (James 1:17), he heals through doctors, teaches through teachers, creates works of beauty through artists, and makes our earthly life easier through scientists, engineers, and inventors.

God, out of his love and goodness, freely distributes such gifts to everyone whom he has created, Christian and non-Christian, good and evil, just and unjust (Matt. 5:45). And he bestows such gifts through everyone whom he has created, the just and the unjust. Was the farmer who grew the grain that went into the piece of toast I ate this morning a Christian? I hope so, but even if he was not, God nourished me through him. By the same token it is possible to learn from someone who is a non-Christian. After all, the talents, knowledge, and skills necessary for each particular vocation are themselves gifts of God. Thus we can benefit from those gifts, even if the person who has received them is in rebellion against the Giver.

To be sure, that rebellion can twist those talents, knowledge, and skills. God's divinely appointed purpose for all vocations is to use them as means of loving and serving our neighbors. But it is also possible to misuse our vocations to harm, deceive, and exploit our neighbors. Yet God can use those whom he has called and equipped despite themselves to accomplish his purpose.

When we walk through the Areopagus of today's world we will find much of value, but, like Paul, we will also see one idol after another. The same can be said of reading through the great books of Western civilization, or of taking a philosophy survey course, or of walking through an art museum, or of surfing the Internet.

What are we to make of the sequence of worldviews that are arrayed against those set forth in Scripture? Can we learn from them, or must we reject them entirely? If we see each worldview merely as its own self-contained system, how can we prevent the biblical worldview from being reduced to just one of many views of the world, with all being equally valid? This sounds suspiciously like the contemporary worldview of postmodernism. How can we avoid the impression that truth is relative and insist instead on the transcendent truth of God's Word?

Consider this overview of the major movements of Western thought: From the 1000s through the 1600s, that is, the Middle

Ages through the Reformation, a Christian worldview shaped the ideas, art, and culture of the times. (Notice that people with radically different theologies can nevertheless share a Christian worldview.) Then came the Enlightenment in the 1700s, the Age of Reason. But the first half of the nineteenth century saw a reaction against reason and the rise of Romanticism, the Age of Emotion. With the 1850s and the rise in science and industrialism came the dominance of scientific materialism. The first half of the twentieth century was the age both of modernism, with its faith in progress, and of the disillusionment of existentialism. Then came postmodernism, which gave up on progress, reason, and objective truth.

Instead of seeing Christianity as offering just one worldview among many, we must think of Christianity as being bigger, more complex, and more comprehensive than the others are. Indeed, Christianity has a place for reason *and* emotion *and* the material realm *and* what is new *and* existential angst *and* skepticism about the achievements of man *and* the limits of reason.

We can see the different worldviews as pieces of truth torn from the seamless garment that is the Christian faith and in many cases fashioned into an idol. But a Christian can learn about reason from Enlightenment authors while also learning about emotion from the Romantics. Christians can appreciate natural science and make use of technology. But they also know its limits. They can relate to the tortured existentialist and agree with the postmodernist about the failures of modernism and the limits of the human mind.

Ironically, the secularist who is committed to one of these worldviews *cannot* appreciate or learn from the others. A devotee of the Enlightenment believes that reason is the *only* way to approach reality, scorning emotion just as a Romantic lives *only* for emotion and reacts against rationalism. Modernists end up rejecting virtually everything in the past, everything that is not new. Postmodernists have more sympathy with the past, except for the more recent past of modernism.

Christians, on the other hand, can draw from them all without succumbing completely to any of them. A Christian facing a philosophy that says that man is nothing more than a brute animal can say, "Yes, human beings are limited, sinful, and depraved. . . . But human beings are also valuable and capable of great things." A Christian facing a humanist can agree that humans are valuable and capable of great things, while at the same time insisting that humans are limited, sinful, and depraved. The Christian worldview paints a much bigger picture of humans than any of the reductive human perspectives. Human beings were made in the image of God and yet are fallen. Between those poles, both of which are affirmed in Scripture, the partial human philosophies all lie.

As G. K. Chesterton has observed, Christianity tends to say, "both/and" (Christ is both God and man, Christians are both sinners and saints, man is both the image of God and fallen, the physical realm both is good and yet passes away).[8] This allows Christians to say, "Yes, but . . ." to the partial discoveries of human beings.

Thus, the great modernist poet T. S. Eliot struggled with the fragmentation that he found in modern life. He decried what he called the "dissociation of sensibility" that has reigned since the Enlightenment, in which thinking and feeling are in conflict with each other.[9] He noted, however, that Christian poets such as John Donne "feel their thought" and think their feelings.[10] Eliot came to realize that the wholeness of sensibility that he craved came from the Christian faith.

About the same time C. S. Lewis wrote about his conversion to Christianity in a story entitled *The Pilgrim's Regress: An Allegorical Apology for Christianity, Reason, and Romanticism.* He saw that in his time both reason *and* romanticism were under attack. To be sure, both attacked Christianity, though for opposite reasons (because it contains supernatural mysteries and because it contains objective doctrines), but Lewis found that Christianity preserves and offers a basis for both the life of the mind and the experience of the heart.

Again, Christianity is bigger than all the humanly devised worldviews. These do typically have a reason for coming into existence (the bloody religious fanaticism of the Thirty Years' War led to the reaction of Enlightenment rationalism, the aridity of reason alone led to the reaction of recovering the inner life, and so on). The problem is that these different emphases are so easily turned into all-encompassing ideologies. Christianity, on the other hand, offers a framework for being open to truth, goodness, and beauty (to draw on the "absolutes" of classical philosophy) wherever they are found, while also being critical (a prerequisite of modern and postmodern scholarship).[11]

Christians then can say with the psalmist "Great are the works of the LORD, studied by all who delight in them" (Ps. 111:2). It is right to "delight" in the works of the Lord, which encompass everything that exists. And that delight makes us want to study them, to know God's works as fully and as deeply as we can—to the limits of our perception and our thinking. The psalmist concludes with the perspective that makes this possible: "The fear of the LORD is the beginning of wisdom; all those who practice it have a good understanding" (111:10).

For Discussion

1. How does the understanding that Christ is Lord of "all things" inform our attitude toward the writings of the unregenerate?

2. Though Christ is Lord of all things, sin nevertheless infects both the writer and the reader. How then may we sort out what is true and praiseworthy?

3. What are the dangers of reading or viewing or experiencing works that are well produced but not biblical?

4. How might the writings and works of nonbelievers be a source of moral education?

5. What does the author mean when he offers, "Instead of seeing Christianity as offering just one worldview among many, we must think of Christianity as being bigger, more complex, and more comprehensive than the others are"?

6. Is there a work by a non-Christian—a writing, art, or film—that impacted you in a positive way?

7. Can you think of a work that expresses biblical truth, although the writer is not a Christian believer?

8

Hardwired for Pleasure

Paul David Tripp

The heavens declare the glory of God,
　　and the sky above proclaims his handiwork.
Day to day pours out speech,
　　and night to night reveals knowledge.
There is no speech, nor are there words,
　　whose voice is not heard.
Their voice goes out through all the earth,
　　and their words to the end of the world.
In them he has set a tent for the sun,
　　which comes out like a bridegroom leaving his chamber,
　　and, like a strong man, runs its course with joy.
Its rising is from the end of the heavens,
　　and its circuit to the end of them,
　　and there is nothing hidden from its heat. (Ps. 19:1–6)

As for the rich in this present age, charge them not to be haughty, nor to set their hopes on the uncertainty of riches, but on God, who richly provides us with everything to enjoy. (1 Tim. 6:17)

If someone asked you what the biggest word in the Bible was, what would you answer? Don't think too hard; the answer is quite obvious. Although it is made up of only five letters, there is no word in the Bible as big as the word *grace*. This gargantuan

121

word spreads its meaning and influence over literally every page of Scripture. It isn't enough to say that the Bible talks a lot about grace. It isn't enough to say that the Bible carefully develops a theology of grace. It's not enough to say that the Bible promotes a lifestyle with grace at the center. No, you have to say that grace is what the Bible is *about*. The Bible unfolds to you and to me God's grand story of grace. The Bible is at its core a great big grace story. Maybe it would be best to say the Bible is an annotated grace story—that is, it is a grace story with God's essential explanatory notes.

Now this word *grace* is such a big container that even the world of pleasure fits inside it. Maybe you're thinking, "Paul, what in the world does pleasure have to do with grace?" The answer is, "Everything." One of the ways God showers us with his day-by-day grace is by placing us in a world where pleasure is a daily gift, and because it is, it is also a daily personal experience.

A beautiful piece of music
The smell of a sizzling steak
The delicate fluff of the clouds
The beauty of the daffodil
The tenderness of a human kiss
The silvery, glistening sheen of a newly frozen pond
The repeating song of the bird
The juice of a ripe apple, squirting down your throat
The visual wonder of a great painting
The sedentary joy of sleep
The cool refreshment of water
The delightful sting of the red pepper on your tongue
The harmonious voices of a well-rehearsed choir
The deep moan of a stringed bass
The endless variety of human clothing
The wide catalog of ethnic cuisines
The evening sun resting on the horizon
White stone cliffs falling down to the deep blue sea

The coat of the tiger
The silly antics of the monkey
The gripping drama of a good novel or movie
The quick wit of a skilled comedian
The artful palate of a great chef
The joy of the love of another
The security of the touch of a loved one's hand

These are but a few of the daily pleasures that are not only part of our lives, but part of our lives because God is so grand, good, wise, faithful, loving, and giving in his grace. In a world completely devoid of God's grace, none of these things would exist. Without his grace life would be bleak, dark, and boring. Our lives would be a sad, lonely walk through an unending and unfulfilling void. No grace, no pleasure—that is the bottom line. If you know and love God, if you get who he is, and if you want to live as he intended, then you should live a pleasurable life, and you should not be ashamed that you do. Pleasure came from him. Pleasure belongs to him. Pleasure is one of his gifts of grace to you. Pleasure exists for your good and his glory. If you are God's child, no one should enjoy pleasure as it was meant to be enjoyed more than you. Let me explain.

God's Grace and Your Pleasure

I thoroughly enjoy and am very thankful for the symphony of pleasures that are all around me. I participate in many of those pleasures, and I am not ashamed that I do. You should enjoy them too and not feel guilty that you do. But to help you fully understand what I have just confessed and to keep you from being afraid that I have gone off the deep end, you and I need to examine the Bible's theology of pleasure.

God in Grace Created Pleasure

You and I are surrounded by so much pleasure that it is easy to forget how much pleasure God has graciously given us.

So it is important to stop, look, and listen once again. When it comes to pleasure, the place to begin looking is the garden of Eden. The garden was a beautiful place, so beautiful that the Creator could stand back and say it was "very good." It was perfect in every way. God placed what seemed to be an endless variety of plants and animals in the garden, all bringing with them a wide catalog of sights, sounds, and smells. There were pleasures everywhere you looked. There was more beauty than your eyes could take in. It was a wonderful, beautiful, pleasurable place. The garden of Eden was beautiful and jam-packed with pleasure because that is exactly how God wanted it to be.

You will simply never, ever have pleasure in its proper place in your life; you will never be able to enjoy it as God meant for it to be enjoyed; and you will never keep it from controlling you as it has the power to do unless you start here: God created pleasure. Pleasure is not a human invention. It is not the creation of the Epicureans. All forms of rightful pleasure came out of the mind of God and are consistent with his purpose for his creation and for the creatures made in his image. By God's design, pleasure is not a bad thing, an evil thing, a dark thing, a shameful thing, or a thing to be avoided. Pleasure is the gift of a loving, wise, and gracious God, and because it is, you don't have to feel ashamed that you like pleasure. God likes pleasure and he wired you to like it too. So it is not godly to avoid pleasure as if it were innately evil. A pleasureless existence does not bring you closer to God. God is the Creator of pleasure and the Creator of the physical world, which is the delivery system of that pleasure. Pleasure exists because God exists and has wired pleasure into the world he so wisely constructed.

God in Grace Hardwired You for Pleasure

For the purposes of this chapter, this second point is as important as the first. It is not enough to say that God created pleasure and that he made a world that is jam-packed with it. It is not enough to say that you wake up every morning to a world of amazing beauty of sight, sound, touch, smell, and taste. It is not enough to say that God as Creator exposes everyone to that beauty whether they deserve it or not (and no one does). Something else fundamental and important needs to be said. Here it is: God designed you for pleasure. Both your inner man (your heart) and your outer man (your body) have been hard-wired for pleasure. You are drawn to pleasure as the result of God's good, gracious, and wise design.

First, God placed in your heart a desire for pleasure. Every human being is drawn toward pleasure. Every human being is motivated to find and experience pleasure. Every person who has ever lived finds pleasure pleasurable. You love the world around you with its variegated tastes, its symphony of sounds, and its smorgasbord of smells. You love being entertained. You love the great painting and that first summer hot dog. You love hearing a great piece of music, and you love having your back scratched. You love being blown away by a grand piece of archi-tecture, and you love playing with your hopelessly loyal dog. Admit it; you don't need to be ashamed. You desire pleasure; you hope for it every day; and you do because your Creator placed pleasure orientation in your heart. But not only have you been created with a pleasure orientation (in your inner man), you have been designed with pleasure receptors (on your outer man).

It is not just people who are right with God, and righteous in his eyes, who have been given pleasure receptors. You and I were not put on pleasure-receptor probation until we earned the right to enjoy the pleasures that have been wired into the physical world around us. No, our capacity to recognize, take in, and enjoy pleasure is a gift of God's grace. You and I enjoy this gift even on our worst, most rebellious day. That is how great God's grace is. You have just been impatient with your wife, but you walk outside and your eyes are filled with the beauty of the dogwoods in bloom. How great is God's grace. You lashed out at your coworker, spilling bitterness you have carried for months, yet that day at lunch your taste buds still work and remind you how good pizza really is. How great is God's grace. You just cut off another driver in your haste to get to your destination; meanwhile your ears are filled with the pounding beat of the music on your car's sound system. How great is God's grace. You're angry because the bicycle is lying in the driveway as usual, but you can't wait to get in the house and sample the cookies you bought because the smell has been driving you crazy on the way home. How great is God's grace.

In bountiful love and patient grace, God gives us the ability to take in the pleasures of the physical world around us, not because of who we are but because of who he is. He graces us with everything from friendships to flowers, from mountains to music, and from the pleasures of love to the delights of food. And he gives us the capacity to enjoy them all. In grace he really did hardwire us not only with the desire for pleasure, but with highly specified and integrated receptors to take in the pleasures that our hearts desire.

God in Grace Has Told Us That Pleasure Requires Boundaries

God knows how pleasing pleasure can be because he created pleasure, but he also knows that pleasure carries with it dangers as well. When something pleases you, it is natural to want more. This is the danger of pleasure. The danger of pleasure comes from the fact that it is pleasurable. Your tongue tastes chocolate and sends a message to your brain, "More of this, please," and your brain sends a message to your hand, "Put more of this in his mouth," and the cycle repeats. You simply cannot allow yourself to follow pleasure's draw. That is why Scripture warns us not to "love the world or the things in the world" (1 John 2:15). It warns us to be careful not to make a god out of our stomach (Phil. 3:19). Pleasure without boundaries becomes dark and dangerous. You don't need to go any further than to hear the instructions God gives Adam and Eve in the garden or to see what happens when they step outside the boundaries that God set for them.

Sex is a wonderful God-given pleasure, but only when enjoyed inside the clear boundaries that God has set. Food is beautiful to see, smell, and taste, but you cannot eat whatever you want whenever you want, so God warns us against gluttony. Money can be a doorway to wonderful pleasures, but the Bible warns us not to give the love of our hearts to money. Physical possessions can bring you much pleasure, but God warns us against living for the purpose of piling up earthly treasures. Relationships are a beautiful thing, but Scripture warns against putting people in God's place.

You see, it is quite clear that for pleasure to be pleasurable and not harmful, boundaries are required. So God not only graces us with pleasure and hardwires us to enjoy that pleasure, he also set boundaries for us so we will not be harmed by what he means for us to enjoy. If you let your heart and hands go wherever pleasure leads you, you will end up fat, addicted, and in debt. Because you pursued pleasure without boundaries, what was once pleasing will have morphed into misery. God's restrictions on our pleasure are themselves a grace. And not only are those restrictions found in the Bible, they are wired into creation. You eat too much and you get sick. You eat too much repeatedly and you get fat. You drink too much and you get drunk. You spend too much and you end up in debt. In grace God has even embedded warnings into the way creation operates to remind us that pleasure requires boundaries.

God in Grace Created Pleasure So All Pleasure Would Point to Him

Here is the bottom line—in grace God infused pleasure with purpose. The end of pleasure is not pleasure. All the pleasures of the created world are a means to an end, and the end is that the awe-inspiring, mind-bending, heart-stopping grandeur and glory of God would be seen and heard by creatures created for the sole purpose of relationship with him. You see, if you don't understand that the end of pleasure is not pleasure, you will look to pleasure to get the one thing that pleasure can never ever give you—life. Pleasure is wonderful, but it is not ultimate. The God who created pleasure is ultimate. Pleasure is a wonderful part of life, but it is not life-giving. Pleasure offers you momentary joy, but it has no capacity whatsoever to bring satisfaction and peace to your heart.

So, why did God create pleasure, why did he give us the capacity to experience it, and why does he put so many pleasures in our path? Sure he did it because he is tender and kind and wants life to be enjoyable for us, but there is much more. God designed the pleasures of this physical created world to be one big finger that points to him. He did this because he knows that we have the perverse ability to forget and ignore him. So in grace, he created pleasures that would point to him and reveal his character so that we would acknowledge him and our need of him. All of this is so that we would run to him in submission, thanks, and worship. The pleasures of this world and our ability to take them in are all part of God's grand mission of rescuing, forgiving, and transforming, and of delivering grace. He graces us with pleasure so that we will run after the ultimate pleasure of knowing, loving, serving, and worshiping him. God employs the most common aspects of his every-day, every-person grace as tools of the saving grace that every person so desperately needs. Now that is grace!

Your Enjoyment of Pleasure Brings God Pleasure

Your enjoyment of pleasure is not necessarily worldly. It is not something that should make you feel guilty. It is not something that should be shrouded in shame. Pleasure is God's idea. Your attraction to pleasure is God's idea. Putting pleasure before your eyes is God's idea. Your pleasure sensitivity is God's idea. It all exists for his glory. Pleasure, in and of itself, is not dark and dangerous. Pleasure is not a bad thing. It is a good and

God-glorifying thing when it is enjoyed as God intended and is inside the boundaries he has clearly laid down.

If pleasure brings God glory, then God is pleased by your enjoyment of the pleasure that he has graciously blessed you with. God is pleased whenever you celebrate his blessings and give thanks for the bounty of his grace. So go out and enjoy. Smile, sing, and celebrate. Take a photograph of something beautiful. Cook a wonderful meal. Savor the roast beef sandwich and let the ice cream cone drip down on your hand. Take in a great concert. Go to the opera or a Broadway play. Repaint and redecorate your living room. Curl up with your iPad and a new novel. Peel that succulent orange and smile. Get physical with your spouse and enjoy it. Let that candy bar remind you of how good chocolate really is. As long as you stay inside God's boundaries, not only can you do it all without guilt, you can do it all as an act of worship. Celebrate the glory of God that is revealed in every pleasure that he created and chooses for you to encounter. God is pleased when you are pleased by what he has blessed you with, particularly when you recognize that it has come from his gracious hands.

Sin Makes Pleasure Dangerous

Pleasure is not what makes pleasure dangerous—sin is. Now prepare to have your feelings hurt. The greatest dangers in the world of pleasure are to be found inside of you, not outside of you. Sex is not dangerous, but your lust is. Food is not dangerous, but your gluttony is. Money is not dangerous, but your greed is. Enjoyment of pleasure is not dangerous, but your addiction is. The sin that you bring to pleasure poisons pleasure and makes it a deadly thing.

Sin does evil with what God intended to be good. Sin pollutes God's good gifts of grace. Sin alters and distorts our whole relationship with the world of pleasure because sin changes us. Sin captures the thoughts and desires of our hearts, and in so doing fundamentally changes the way we deal with the pleasures God created for our good and for his glory.

It really is true that pleasure is not the problem, sin is. This is precisely why the ascetic environment of the medieval monastery did not work. What was the theology of the monastery? Well, it went something like this: there is an evil world out there, so the way to escape evil is to build a big wall and separate yourself from the world. We all know that monasteries replicated all the evils of the surrounding world. They failed because they located the source of the problem in the wrong place. The problem was not the world and its pleasures. Those pleasures don't cause you to sin, and separating yourself from them won't cause you to be righteous. No, what causes me to use the pleasures in a way that God calls evil is the sin inside of me. Sin causes me to use sinfully what God designed to be a blessing.

Sin causes me to put myself in the center of my world. Sin reduces the scope of my motivations and concerns to the small confines of what I want, what I feel, what pleases me, and what I think I need. Sin really does make life all about me. In that way sin makes me ravenous, greedy, selfish, demanding, entitled, discontent, and envious. Sin causes my appetite for pleasure to be unrestrained and unlimited. I want what I want, I want it how I want it and where I want it, I want it now, and I want it in the biggest portions possible. Do you see what's happening here? Sin causes me to replace the love I should have for God with the love of personal pleasure. Sin causes me to resist any boundaries or restraints placed on me. Sin causes me to want to use what I want to use in the way that I want to use it. Sin makes me a danger to myself and causes me to poison God's world of pleasure with wrong motives and selfish desires. Sin causes me to ignore the One who is the author and giver of pleasure. It causes me to make the very pleasures that were made to point to him to instead be all about me.

The fact that I have any pleasure in my life at all is an argument for God's grace, but I need grace in order to be able to use these gifts of grace in the way that he intended. No, I don't so much need to be rescued from pleasure. I need to be rescued from me, so that I am able to enjoy the pleasures I have been given in a way that pleases the Giver.

When It Comes to Pleasure You Must Worship the Giver and Not the Gift

In grace God uses the pleasures of the world he created to expose the deepest struggle of the human heart. The deepest struggle of the human heart is not about how much you have suffered or how much pleasure you have been allowed to enjoy. No, the deepest, most important, long-term struggle of every human's heart is the struggle of worship. The question of questions is, "Will our lives be shaped by the worship of the one who is Creator and Controller of all things, or will we exchange worship of him for worship of what he created?" Let me put this in pleasure language for you. Will you give your heart to be ruled by the love of pleasure, or will your heart be ruled by the Creator and Giver of pleasure? Will you worship the gift or the Giver?

Whether you realize it or not your life is always shaped by the worship of something or someone. You are always attaching your identity, your definition of meaning and purpose, and your inner sense of well-being to something. You are always seeking to find life. This means you are always looking for life horizontally or vertically. You are asking created things to satisfy your searching heart, or you have realized that physical things can never satisfy your heart but rather are there to point you to the One who alone is able to give your heart peace and rest. God in grace uses the pleasures of the created world to expose the idolatry of my fickle heart. While I functionally forget him, I tell myself that I would be satisfied if only I had _____.

So God uses the pleasures that are all around me not only to bless me with an interesting and enjoyable life, but to remind me of how deep my need is for his rescuing grace. Pleasure exposes how I turn the desire and enjoyment of a good thing into a bad thing because I have allowed it to become a ruling thing. How amazing it is that the good gift of pleasure is used by God to help me to see my need for an even better gift—the gift of his forgiving and rescuing grace.

If You Are God's Child, You Are Headed for Pure Pleasure Forevermore

This chapter has celebrated God's gracious gift of pleasure, the gift that makes our lives enjoyable, interesting, and engaging even on the days when we are rebellious and unthankful. God's common grace of pleasure reminds us that no one ever faces a day devoid of his grace; his grace shines through the sun, is whispered by the wind, and comes wafting to us in the smells of spring. The fact that he showers beauty down on us is not an endorsement of who we are and what we are doing, rather it is a global revelation of who he is. You cannot look out your window or walk out your door without seeing grace. Open your senses to the sight, sound, touch, taste, and smell world of pleasure, and remember that each pleasure points you to One of unlimited glory and grace.

And there is more to be said. God not only created a world of pleasure for you here and now despite this world's brokenness, but he will also one day welcome each of his children to a world of untold beauty and endless pleasure. You could argue that the biblical story begins in a garden of untainted beauty and pleasure and ends in a city of perfect beauty and pleasure. The beauty of the garden is a sign of God's grace, the journey from garden to city is a story of God's grace, and the final destination of pleasure forever is there only because of his grace.

It is impossible for me to write what I have written here without ending with one of the most glorious and encouraging passages in the Bible.

You make known to me the path of life;
    in your presence there is fullness of joy;
    At your right hand are pleasures forevermore. (Ps. 16:11)

Each phrase of this psalm bursts with meaning.

"You make known to me the path of life." You see, for all its multifaceted delights, pleasure cannot give you life. It is vital to recognize this. Life is never found in the gift; it is only ever found in the Giver.

"In your presence there is fullness of joy." The pleasures of the physical world are temporarily enjoyable, but the shelf life of their enjoyment is short. The taste of food is wonderful, but it does not linger long on your tongue. The delight of musical creativity is enjoyable, but the notes do not ring in your ears for very long. You sit on the edge of your seat during that powerful movie, but on the way home you are already planning for your next day at work. Pleasure is pleasurable, but the pleasures of this right-here, right-now created world can never give you fullness of joy. God graces you with pleasure not to satisfy your heart, but to point you to where your searching heart will finally be satisfied. Joy is found in pleasure, but fullness of joy is to be found only in the One who created pleasure for your good and his glory.

"At your right hand are pleasures forevermore." There's the destination. We will sit with him, and we will reign with him, and, having defeated the last enemy, he will bless us with pleasures beyond our imagination forever and ever and ever. Remember, every pleasure you have experienced so far has been a less-than-perfect pleasure, the product of a terribly broken world. Think of the enjoyments that are before you in a world that has been completely restored and is perfect in every way. And consider that in that place, with all its untold glories, the

thing that will please your heart the most is that by grace you have been welcomed into his presence forever.

For Discussion

1. To enjoy pleasure, why is it critical to understand that God created pleasure?

2. Why is it critical to understand that God has "hardwired" us to receive pleasure?

3. Why are boundaries essential to enjoying pleasure? Can you recount an episode of going beyond the boundaries?

4. According to the author, what is God's purpose for pleasure?

5. Do you agree with the author that God takes pleasure in our taking pleasure even in things that are not religious?

6. The author makes a list of things that give him pleasure. What would be on your list?

7. What makes pleasure dangerous?

8. What can pleasure be turned into?

9. What are the eternal pleasures that you look forward to?

9

The "Good" Neighbor

D. Marion Clark

I HAVE A PROBLEM with my neighbors. Whenever I see them, they smile and warmly greet me. If I express any kind of a need, they are quick to offer help. Several times the wife has brought me and my wife home-cooked meals. They are the models of hospitality. They are, in truth, blessings in my life. All the more, then, I have a problem with them.

You see, they are not Christians. They are Iranians, who, the best I can tell, would lean toward their Persian heritage of Zoroastrianism if they had to be labeled religiously. If they speak of God, it is more in the sense of our quasi-religious American neighbors who believe in a good God who sees the best in everyone.

My problem is this: How do I reconcile that my neighbors, whom I love because they are loveable, will be condemned to hell if they never come to faith? Do I dare to ask the real question, "Shall not the Judge of all the earth do what is just?" (Gen. 18:25). Or if I must accept that condemnation is just, then shall not the Creator of all the earth show mercy? Shall he not at the very least take into account mitigating circumstances or that some sinners are not as wicked as others? For such questions, common grace serves as the best guide to understanding.

God's Mercy

Common grace is God's mercy to the unregenerate. As explained in the two chapters defining common grace, there are two aspects of such grace. One is that God restrains the degree of wickedness in the unregenerate. Thus, the unregenerate is not as bad as his heart would lead him, because God restrains his wicked impulses. God is merciful. He stops the unregenerate person from plunging further into sin before he hurts himself. He monitors the sinful indulgences of the unsaved heart, keeping it from ruin before its time. Like the police officer who hails a cab for the staggering drunk before he gets into trouble, God kindly prevents sin in the unregenerate, as well as the trouble that sin causes, from getting worse. The other aspect of common grace is that God induces good thought and behavior in the unregenerate. He is not merely restraining their wicked impulses but is working in them in such a way that they think and do good things. He grants such grace because he is merciful even to unrepentant sinners.

One might counter that it is a thin mercy in that the unregenerate will suffer nonetheless. The day of judgment will come. It is like helping a man to kick his smoking habit while he awaits execution. Perhaps, but if the condemned prisoner actually does experience better health before his execution, then he would regard that as a mercy nevertheless. It is better to experience some well-being before dying than to feel miserable to the very end.

It is merciful that the wicked are not made to be miserable from the day they are born. And the worst misery is to be a miserable person. We all know of such individuals. Not only are they not happy, they seem to be intent on making everyone else unhappy. It is painful to be a person who inflicts pain; it is miserable to spread misery; and it is the height of unhappiness to express unhappiness.

But God is merciful, and he grants those who ought to be in misery and be miserable the mercy of experiencing blessings and being blessings. Misery should be the lot of all who do not know him. But God grants common grace blessings to the evil and the unjust, so much so that their lives are not only tolerable but in a sense blessed.

In Matthew 5:45, Jesus speaks specifically of the sun and rain that God gives. Such external blessings make people feel good. We know that when people feel good—when their physical and emotional needs are met—they tend to be better persons. But God goes further in his mercy. For he not only gives external common grace blessings that influence the unrighteous heart toward some good, but he directly stirs that heart to do good despite its true nature. We see this played out in otherwise wicked individuals who can be kind.

We regard such persons as complex. They are the ones who make the best material for stories, such as the characters in *The Sopranos*. Indeed, the best storytellers are the ones who bring out both the good and the bad of their characters so that we regard them as truly human, truly like ourselves.

Jesus characterizes us in this way. Elsewhere in his Sermon on the Mount, while teaching how God our Father answers our requests, he reasons that if even we who are evil know how to give good gifts to our children, we can trust our heavenly Father all the more to give good things. When they are unregenerate, our hearts can be designated only as evil. But then why do we not do only what is evil? Because of the good that remains in our hearts? Is it that some of the unregenerate have done a better job than others have (even than some regenerate persons have) of making the most of that good? Or is it more likely that God in his mercy has made his sun's rays to shine on the hearts of the unregenerate and has sent nurturing rain to those same hearts so as to provide a measure of good intentions and actions? The result is that both the unregenerate and the regenerate vary in terms of their dispositions—whether bad or good.

We all know the nice individual, the person who by nature is kind and considerate. These people's nature seems to have nothing to do with their relationship with God. Many are religious, but many are not. They simply have a pleasant disposition. Why are they like that? Immediately people will discuss whether the cause is nature or nurture. No one attributes being nice or mean to autonomous self-will.

No one is autonomous in the sense of exhibiting behavior that is free of internal and external factors beyond his control. What we all have is what has been given to us. We may speak of what we make out of our circumstances, but even then the behaviorist can explain why we respond the way we do.

All of this is to say what the Christian has all along known: God is in control. He is the sovereign Lord who carries out his will, whether it be in the grand scope of history or in the individual life. His Spirit operates in whom he wishes and for whatever purpose he wishes. He operates in whatever means he determines. This includes controlling genetic makeup and environmental influences. It also includes his mysterious interaction with the human heart. He is not limited to the special grace work of salvation and of causing a heart to be regenerated.

So God may grant the common grace blessing of being able to act kindly and appreciate kindness. He may grant the unregenerate mind to perceive that it is better to give than to receive. He may bless the spiritually dead heart with belief in a benevolent creator. He may even give the spiritually blind mind the perception of what is good, even what is holy. He does not have to do so. He could leave the spiritually dead without any faculty for perceiving and exhibiting what is good. It is because he is kind to the ungrateful and to the evil that he grants that even they may exhibit some measure of feeling grateful and doing good.

If we could see what each person is like when stripped of common grace blessings, we would be horrified by the nakedness of the unregenerate heart. William Golding's novel *Lord of the Flies* illustrates this concept. He tells the story of what happens to a group of British boys marooned on an island away from civilization. Once the restraint of living in a civilized society is removed, the savage nature (the heart) of the boys comes out. The book's lesson is that "the beast," thought to be out there, external to the human heart, is within all along.

Civilization is itself a common grace blessing, but more to the point is that common grace works directly on the heart. Even in the novel, the author presents the varying degrees of good and bad in these characters who are experiencing the same circumstance. So we are always coming back to the same questions: Why are some people nicer than others? Why do some individuals display more good than others? What accounts for the variation? What accounts for any unregenerate heart displaying good will?

The only answer comes when we return to the source, namely, the grace of God granting the blessings of kindness. Why does God do this? Why doesn't he operate in a clean pattern in which the unregenerate grow increasingly wicked and the regenerate increasingly good? There may very well be such a pattern, which the God who knows all human hearts sees clearly. Even we who are regenerate see only as though in a mirror dimly. No doubt when the day of judgment comes and justice is meted out, we will see the wisdom and justice of God's actions.

It is not difficult to see some reasoning even now for what appears to be an indiscriminate scattering of common grace blessings. For one thing, such blessings serve to humble the regenerate. The good actions of my unregenerate neighbors confront my deficiencies in the same areas. Far from saying, "There but by the grace of God go I," I challenge myself, "Why, by the grace of God, have I not progressed there?" Such neighbors keep me from ever thinking that I was saved because of my goodness or that becoming saved has automatically made me superior. Because God gives the unregenerate common grace gifts of intellect and even moral character, I am refrained from presumptuously believing that I and my fellow regenerated believers must always be in the right.

These seemingly indiscriminate blessings bestowed on the unregenerate also end up blessing me. My life is made more pleasant because of the good nature of my neighbors. My overall quality of life is raised because God has endowed unregenerate people with gifts to invent and produce products that benefit mankind. My life is safer because he has induced courage, patriotism, protective instincts, and other honorable qualities in men and women who have gone their own way from God.

And this leads to another reason for common grace. By such work God displays all the more his power and sovereignty. We know that through redemptive grace God delights in saving the foolish and weak so as to shame the wise and the strong of the world. Through common grace he achieves the same end by using the very persons who would deny him as God to do his bidding.

What common grace most teaches the regenerate is that God our Father is kind—he is kind to the ungrateful and the evil, and therefore so should we be. These are good lessons to learn, however perplexed I may be about the patterns God uses to teach them.

But what should common grace teach the unregenerate? Or the more pointed question is, what does common grace reveal about the true nature of the unregenerate? Jesus put his finger on it—at heart they are ungrateful and evil (as we were without redemptive grace). We struggle most with the part about being evil, because we cannot see this evil or at least see it at its full extent. I can think of no one in my personal experience whom I would classify as an evil person. But, as already noted, it is common grace that restrains and mitigates evil so that it is not fully realized or displayed.

For me to complain about God punishing one whom he deems evil because I could not see his true nature would be the same as criticizing a doctor for subjecting a loved one of mine to painful medical treatment because I could not see the cancer ravaging through the body. Jack Nicholson is right: I can't handle the truth—not the truth of evil within me or anyone else I know.

But I can see evidence of that other characterization that Jesus made, namely, that of being ungrateful. God the Father bestows blessing upon blessing on the unregenerate, who respond in one of two fashions: either they do not acknowledge God as Giver or, if they do, they believe that those blessings signify God's approval of them.

Consider the first response—or, more accurately stated, lack of response. Our kind neighbors credit themselves with their kindness. Our neighbors who do good deeds regard their works as springing from their naturally good hearts. Our neighbors who act courageously for justice and for the needy believe in themselves. That, of course, is what the world teaches. Believe in yourself. Recognize that your own heart is good. And, if there is a God, know that God (however you may conceive him to be) is pleased with you as you are.

Scripture labels this attitude as idolatry and pride.

> For the wrath of God is revealed from heaven against all ungodliness and unrighteousness of men, who by their unrighteousness suppress the truth. For what can be known about God is plain to them, because God has shown it to them. For his invisible attributes, namely, his eternal power and divine nature, have been clearly perceived, ever since the creation of the world, in the things that have been made. So they are without excuse. For although they knew God, they did not honor him as God or give thanks to him, but they became futile in their thinking, and their foolish hearts were darkened. Claiming to be wise, they became fools, and exchanged the glory of the immortal God for images resembling mortal man and birds and animals and creeping things. (Rom. 1:18–23)

The unregenerate are quick to ask why being acknowledged would matter so much to God. But the real question is why the unregenerate cannot do so simple a thing. Why can they not give God his due? Excuses will be given. How do I know there is a god? Why doesn't he make himself more known? Why should I be punished for lacking belief when I still do good or good enough?

But again, why not believe? Why not give thanks? We make the issue of religious belief more complicated than it is. The Romans passage above says that natural revelation is enough to lead toward belief in the true God and to give thanks to him. But God has also given his revealed Word—the Scriptures of the Bible. It is there to read. God has not hidden himself. He has revealed himself as Creator. He has revealed the problem of sin, which estranges him from his human creatures. He has solved the problem through providing Christ's work of salvation. He has then revealed the answer so that we might avail ourselves of his salvation. Why not believe?

The unregenerate heart will give many reasons why not. Indeed, the unregenerate will devote the intellect they have received through common grace to prove why they should not believe. They will use the gifts of kindness and benevolence as excuses for not having to repent of sin and turn to Christ, which leads to the second class of response—taking God's common grace blessings as signs of his approval of them.

They reason, "God loves us as we are. He is pleased with us; he believes in us—believes that we are at heart good. How do we know? Look at the blessings that he gives us. Would he give us these gifts if he were displeased with us?"

It is such reasoning that motivates the unregenerate to do good. They wish to earn the favor of God. They delight in receiving his gifts that, they reason, come from being good. What have they to do with a gospel that proclaims them to be evil? And how could they ever be accused of being ungrateful when they work all the harder to show their gratefulness and to prove their worthiness of such gifts?

So they fail to see God's common grace gifts for what they truly are—gifts that spring from mercy and kindness, that spring from his character, not theirs. Far from letting them conclude how worthy they must be, his gifts for them ought to have led them to recognize their unworthiness, as George Herbert did in his poem "Love Bade Me Welcome."

Love bade me welcome, yet my soul drew back,
    Guilty of dust and sin.
But quick-ey'd Love, observing me grow slack
    From my first entrance in,
Drew nearer to me, sweetly questioning
    If I lack'd anything.

"A guest," I answer'd, "worthy to be here";
    Love said, "You shall be he."
"I, the unkind, the ungrateful? ah my dear,
    I cannot look on thee."
Love took my hand and smiling did reply,
    "Who made the eyes but I?"

"Truth, Lord, but I have marr'd them; let my shame
    Go where it doth deserve."
"And know you not," says Love, "who bore the blame?"
    "My dear, then I will serve."
"You must sit down," says Love, "and taste my meat."
    So I did sit and eat.[1]

Unlike Herbert, the unregenerate protest that they are kind and grateful. Why else would Love bid them welcome? Again, why else would God the Father send them gifts if he did not already regard them as his beloved children? The unregenerate cannot get into their minds that their hearts are evil. They cannot accept such a thought. It is as blasphemous to them as we would regard ascribing sin to God.

The very reason they cannot comprehend that their hearts are evil is that God, through common grace, has restrained their evil and induced good qualities in them. Thus, they conclude that their hearts are basically good and that sin is the anomaly. "That's not me," they say when they have acted wrong. Circumstances caused them to act out of character, which is a good character. If religious, they might even attribute their wicked impulse to the Devil's influence. Whatever the cause for sinful thought and behavior, it is not to be found in their good heart, notwithstanding Jesus' comment to the contrary.

> What comes out of a person is what defiles him. For from within, out of the heart of man, come evil thoughts, sexual immorality, theft, murder, adultery, coveting, wickedness, deceit, sensuality, envy, slander, pride, foolishness. All these evil things come from within, and they defile a person. (Mark 7:20–23)

The irony of common grace in the life of the unregenerate is that it leads both unregenerate and regenerate to question God's mercy. Out of mercy God gives good gifts to the ungrateful and evil, enough to make them appear better than they are. Because they appear better than they are, we then question how a merciful God could condemn them. And even this reasoning reveals our faulty thinking. What we mean by "mercy" is something that is actually merited because the recipient has demonstrated some good in himself. We do not expect mercy to be shown to the truly wicked. So if God had withheld common grace from the unregenerate, the sinful heart would have developed fully in its terrible nature, and we would not question his justice or mercy.

Hell

Hell is the concept that we would like to do without. One might utter in a moment of anger, "Go to hell," but who would actually assign even an enemy to a punishment that never ends? We can accept punishment that is limited in degree and term. But everlasting torment? It is difficult enough to regard a Hitler assigned to such a fate, but what of the kindly neighbor next door? What of the hero who died saving the lives of others? How could he be sent to torment?

It is a doctrine that gives us pause, we who turned to Christ in the first place so that we might be saved from condemnation. Indeed, the irony for most of us is that what we can accept for ourselves—that our sins deserve condemnation—we have a difficult time accepting for others. Why would that be?

One reason is because of the saving love that we have experienced. The love of God in Christ has made us loving. We have the same perspective as our Father, who said, "Have I any pleasure in the death of the wicked . . . and not rather that he should turn from his way and live?" (Ezek. 18:23). The prospect of hell should cause us to tremble for our unregenerate neighbors. We should not be indifferent to their fate. It should pain us. It should cause us to cry out to God to be merciful. It should move us all the more to take the gospel to everyone.

But is hell real? Let's turn to Jesus, who made the most comments about the subject.

> But I say to you that everyone who is angry with his brother will be liable to judgment; whoever insults his brother will be liable to the council; and whoever says, "You fool!" will be liable to the hell of fire. (Matt. 5:22)

> If your right eye causes you to sin, tear it out and throw it away. For it is better that you lose one of your members than that your whole body be thrown into hell. (Matt. 5:29)

> And do not fear those who kill the body but cannot kill the soul. Rather fear him who can destroy both soul and body in hell. (Matt. 10:28)

> You serpents, you brood of vipers, how are you to escape being sentenced to hell? (Matt. 23:33)

> But I will warn you whom to fear: fear him who, after he has killed, has authority to cast into hell. Yes, I tell you, fear him! (Luke 12:5)

> And in Hades, being in torment, he lifted up his eyes and saw Abraham far off and Lazarus at his side. (Luke 16:23, from the parable of the rich man and Lazarus)

The concept of hell has never been popular, but it has come under even greater skepticism today, if only because some Christian writers have tried to debunk it. That is a natural desire when one has experienced God's love. We don't want anyone to face hell. But will any of us claim to have a love that is greater than our Lord's, a love that led him to literally die as a ransom to save his enemies from hell? It is he who warns of hell. It is he who raises its terrifying specter for the very purpose of terrifying sinners. Is he raising a false bogeyman, as adults will do to frighten children into good behavior? Is he warning us to fear what actually does not exist?

What exactly hell entails is unclear. We do not know specifically what life is like beyond the grave. We have images from Scripture depicting heaven in terms of splendor and delight, and images of hell as the place of torment. It is clear that the Scripture never assures us that hell is not too bad a place or that we won't have to endure it for long or that it is a halfway house that prepares us for heaven. We add those concepts because, well, because everlasting punishment is difficult emotionally to handle.

Let's trust our Lord on this. Whatever hell may be, he thought it necessary to warn us about it as the worst thing that could happen to us. Indeed, it is so terrible that he abandoned heaven, took on our flesh, and died as a sacrifice upon a cross so that we would not face the destiny of hell due to our sins.

It is this redemptive work of Christ that sheds light on the true nature of our sinful hearts no matter how nice common grace may seem to make us, and on the pangs of hell no matter how much our tender feelings wish to mitigate them. It is the redemptive work of Christ that blows away any thought that we might be more loving or more just than God when we contemplate hell and our good neighbors. We would not go through such a sacrifice ourselves. And we who are parents know that the Father's sacrifice in giving up his Son for his enemies was as terrible to bear as the sacrifice that the Son bore, if not more so. No, we do not understand such love; we do not understand the holiness and the righteousness that required such a sin offering; we do not understand the abject slavery into which we were bound that entailed such a ransom.

It is when we forget the cost borne to save sinners that we underestimate the terrible nature of sin. Look to the cross for clarity about man's condition—about every man and woman's condition.

> Ye who think of sin but lightly
> Nor suppose the evil great
> Here may view its nature rightly,
> Here its guilt may estimate.
> Mark the Sacrifice appointed,
> See who bears the awful load;
> 'Tis the Word, the Lord's Anointed,
> Son of Man and Son of God.[2]

Yes, look to the cross and do not tone down or remove hell to salve your tender conscience. Instead, seek the heart of the God who made such a sacrifice to rescue both the "good" and the "bad" neighbor, who have both in truth rebelled against him. Do not spoof hell so that it turns into a mere joke not to be taken seriously. And never be comfortable with it; never be comfortable with the idea that your neighbor or your enemy is destined there unless he or she turns to the Savior who died as his or her ransom.

> O prithee do not callous speak
> About the end of wayward man,
> Who can not, will not, does not seek
> And so beneath His wrath yet stands.
>
> But first a hush should pause your speech,
> A silent tear war with your eyes,
> Towards God a trembling whisper reach
> "Lord help me trust You with these 'Why's!"

For that which breaks the heart of God
Has not left my heart free, untouched,
For I have loved, do love, will love,
Those as yet not turned from such.

Known I the pain of such love, weak,
I might have turned me from this path—
But prithee do not callous speak
Of our beloveds under wrath.[3]

Point them to the cross. Do not let anyone point to their own hearts for their worthiness or salvation.

For Discussion

1. How is common grace God's mercy to the unregenerate?

2. Have you considered how good traits, such as kindness and thankfulness, are themselves the common grace blessings God gives to the otherwise wicked?

3. What neighbors can you think of who have received such blessings?

4. How have these gifts displayed in your unregenerate neighbors served as common grace blessings for you?

5. How do common grace gifts in the unregenerate glorify God?

6. How do the unregenerate abuse their common grace gifts, even those of kindness?

7. What failure distinguishes the good unregenerate from the receiver of special grace?

8. How does the redemptive work of Christ on the cross lead us to a right understanding about hell?

Conclusion

The Limits of Common Grace

D. Marion Clark

WE STARTED WITH A PROBLEM—how to account for good in people whom Scripture declares to be unrighteous. Then we found an answer—that good comes from a benevolent God who grants good gifts even to the wicked. The complex problem has a simple answer—God gets all the credit.

This, simply, is what the doctrine of common grace has to say: to God be all the glory. No one possesses anything that God has not given. No one has taken what was left over after the fall and then made himself into something. Common grace keeps us all humble. For what we possess we must give credit to God, and we must acknowledge that he has been a generous giver to individuals who do not fit our categories of deserving recipients. Is this not good for our spirits as the redeemed? It keeps us from becoming conceited about a presumed favored status, as it impresses on us all the more that there is nothing in ourselves that compelled God to save us, just as there is no observable rhyme or reason to the dispensation of common grace gifts.

The wonder of common grace is that it makes simple what we tend to complicate or over-reason. Take for example what our attitude ought to be toward our neighbors. We tend to size them up according to their potential to become followers of Christ. Indeed, we may even calculate how much love we ought to show or how long we should be friends with them according to their responsiveness to the gospel. We may be willing to go the extra mile because of the possibility that they are among the elect. But common grace teaches a simple motivation. Be merciful to the wicked and loving to our enemies so that we will be like our Father.

> But love your enemies, and do good, and lend, expecting nothing in return, and your reward will be great, and you will be sons of the Most High, for he is kind to the ungrateful and the evil. Be merciful, even as your Father is merciful. (Luke 6:35–36)

Our reasoning would have taken us along a different path. God is holy and righteous. He will judge the wicked; therefore, he could never actually do what is merciful for the wicked, who will not change and whom he will condemn. That is logical, but it is not what Jesus taught. God the Father "is kind to the ungrateful and the evil." What more do we need to know? What other motivation do we need to love every neighbor?

Another example is the light that common grace throws on the ongoing debate of the Christian's and the church's role in society. One trend is to speak in terms of redeeming society or culture. We are to be involved in doing good so as to redeem our culture that it might then glorify God. Churches develop mission statements with the lofty goal of transforming their communities or cities or nations. Otherwise, why get involved in our communities?

I am uneasy when we take a term like *redeem* and use it to mean anything other than Christ's work of redeeming lost sinners. It seems to me that the history of the world, including the church's work of transforming the world's culture, is well represented in the story of Camelot. For a period of time transformation may very well take place, but it is as likely that transformed neighborhoods, cities, and nations will eventually fall. The sin of the unregenerate world will have its way. What then? Did that work of "redemption" mean nothing? If we dedicate ourselves and our churches to transforming society and then society is not transformed, is it wasted effort? It would be if a redeemed society is what God called his people to achieve.

But common grace informs us that our Father "makes his sun rise on the evil and on the good, and sends rain on the just and on the unjust" (Matt. 5:45), even though the sun and the rain produce no lasting fruit in the evil heart or in the unjust community. And so we may shine our lights and send our nourishing rain in our unjust communities simply because it is good to do and because we want to be like our Father. It is enough to be salt and light, knowing that some who experience that salt and light will give glory to our Father, and that some will not now but will end up glorifying our Father on the last day when they must testify to our good deeds. Either way, we are to be sun, rain, salt, and light in imitation of our Father and our Redeemer. We are to be means of common grace ourselves. What more motivation do we need?

With all this said, as helpful a doctrine as common grace may be, let the user beware; there are limits to what common grace accomplishes and even dangers where this simple doctrine can lead us if we are not careful. In the doctrine of common grace we learn that the Spirit of God has granted gifts to the unregenerate to produce works of beauty and even truth. We learn that we may learn from and enjoy such works. But there is a caveat. We need to read the warning labels cautioning us that works can be deceptive. They are good and true only to the extent that they line up with God's standards and truth.

John Calvin, in his *Institutes of the Christian Religion*, has been quoted in this book to support the doctrine of common grace. He also clarifies the limits of common grace gifts in the unregenerate. In "knowing God" and especially in "knowing his

fatherly favor in our behalf, in which our salvation consists . . .
the greatest geniuses are blinder than moles!" He goes on to
explain.

> Certainly I do not deny that one can read competent and apt
> statements about God here and there in the philosophers, but
> these always show a certain giddy imagination. As was stated
> above, the Lord indeed gave them a slight taste of his divin-
> ity that they might not hide their impiety under a cloak of
> ignorance. And sometimes he impelled them to make certain
> utterances by the confession of which they would themselves
> be corrected. But they saw things in such a way that their see-
> ing did not direct them to the truth, much less enable them
> to attain it! They are like a traveler passing through a field at
> night who in a momentary lightning flash sees far and wide,
> but the sight vanishes so swiftly that he is plunged again into
> the darkness of the night before he can take even a step—let
> alone be directed on his way by its help. Besides, although they
> may chance to sprinkle their books with droplets of truth, how
> many monstrous lies defile them! In short, they never even
> sensed that assurance of God's benevolence toward us (without
> which man's understanding can only be filled with boundless
> confusion). Human reason, therefore, neither approaches, nor
> strives toward, nor even takes a straight aim at, this truth: to
> understand who the true God is or what sort of God he wishes
> to be toward us.[1]

To put it in grace terms, the common grace truth that the
unregenerate possess does not bring them into the understanding and belief of special grace truth. The unredeemed
do not understand what it is to be redeemed and therefore
cannot lead us into the beauty and truth that redemption
would have us know. If we are so led by the works of the unregenerate to appreciation of redemptive truth, it is because the
Holy Spirit has granted us the insight to make the application,
not because the unregenerate author or artist or performer
knew what he was doing.

Now here is the catch. If an author through common grace is able to discern some measure of truth, and if he exercises well his common grace gift to write with winsomeness, he may very well lead the undiscerning regenerate reader along stray paths. This book is titled *The Problem of Good*. I came up with the title to address the problem I have with explaining the good in the unregenerate heart. I strongly feel tension after reading a well-crafted book of fiction that presents "good" characters who seem to be good and to do well without God entering the picture, or who have a moralistic perspective of God. When a writer compellingly presents half-truths and insights into human character, I begin to waver. Their viewpoint seems so plausible.

In our openness to learning the truth that is scattered among the unregenerate, in our eagerness to enjoy the pleasures that the unregenerate may produce through the gifts God has granted, we may easily and obliviously follow the path of the unregenerate. We may easily move from being in the world to being of the world. We can learn this lesson from the unregenerate! In *Brave New World*, the humanist writer Aldous Huxley demonstrates how granting pleasurable experience may enslave people who otherwise regard themselves as free. So the world's pleasures and intellectual pursuits may lead the regenerate to be blind to their own captivity to the world. Yes, we may learn from the world; we may enjoy the pleasures produced in the world; but all the more we must be alert to the deceits of the world.

How are we to be alert? If we read the works of the unregenerate, we need to read the works of followers of Christ all the more. We need to worship weekly in the sanctuaries of churches that know the gospel, that proclaim the gospel, that worship God in truth, and whose people testify to the power of the gospel in their lives. We need to make the Bible the book that we read and study daily. The more we understand God's Word and abide by God's Word, the more likely we will be to discern what is true and profitable—and what is false—in the works of the world.

We may very well need to avoid what is lawful because it is not helpful to us. This was the problem of the Corinthians. Exulting in their freedom in Christ, they took on the worst of the world's trappings without benefiting from what may have been used for good. And so they turned whatever wisdom they might have gained from Greek philosophers into opportunities to become puffed up with pride and even to downplay the work of Christ on the cross. They turned even the enjoyment of a good meal into a means to harm the consciences of their brothers and sisters. Sometimes the best action to take for our spiritual welfare is to abstain from things and activities that have moved from legitimate pleasures to idols. I find it necessary to take occasional month-long fasts of otherwise lawful activities in order to break off a dependence that should be reserved only for God and to turn my focus to the gospel.

Another danger is one that John Leonard pointed to (in his chapter on evangelism), and which I did as well (regarding our unregenerate neighbors). The blessings of common grace can lull us into misreading the spiritual condition of the unregenerate. Because an individual seems so good, because he is religious or even God-fearing, we think he is probably accepted by God. That is the very attitude that Romans 2 and 3 addresses. After presenting the downward spiral of the ungodly in chapter 1, the apostle Paul turns to the outwardly religious and moral individuals to warn them of presumption. Far from being set apart from those who do not honor God, they are lumped in with everyone who is a lawbreaker, even with those who do not do good or seek God.

Will we rely on our hearts to discern the hearts of others, or will we rely on the living and active Word of God, which is "sharper than any two-edged sword, piercing to the division of soul and of spirit, of joints and of marrow, and discerning the thoughts and intentions of the heart" (Heb. 4:12)?

This is the warning we must heed for ourselves and about which we should counsel others. Common grace is wonderful indeed, and truly God does display great mercy in bestowing such grace upon the wicked and the ungrateful. Yet to receive such grace without letting it awaken one to the true God, and to one's true condition, comes with a price. As Romans 2:4–5 makes clear,

> Or do you presume on the riches of his kindness and forbearance and patience, not knowing that God's kindness is meant to lead you to repentance? But because of your hard and impenitent heart you are storing up wrath for yourself on the day of wrath when God's righteous judgment will be revealed.

We must not let God's present kindness and patience veil from our eyes his holiness and righteousness, which must see his just wrath eventually realized. Now is the day of salvation; it may not be available tomorrow. Use the common grace blessings to be all the more active in awakening the unregenerate to God's truth.

I've talked about how the doctrine of common grace simplifies complex problems but can also cause confusion in observing hearts—both our own and those of our unregenerate neighbors. There is yet another doctrine that simplifies our understanding of any heart—or, rather, I should say there is a work that puts the heart and everything else in perspective. It is the work of Jesus Christ on the cross.

Romans 3:21–26 succinctly lays forth the plan of salvation.

> But now the righteousness of God has been manifested apart from the law, although the Law and the Prophets bear witness to it—the righteousness of God through faith in Jesus Christ for all who believe. For there is no distinction: for all have sinned and fall short of the glory of God, and are justified by his grace as a gift, through the redemption that is in Christ Jesus, whom God put forward as a propitiation by his blood, to be received by faith. This was to show God's righteousness,

155

> because in his divine forbearance he had passed over former
> sins. It was to show his righteousness at the present time,
> so that he might be just and the justifier of the one who has
> faith in Jesus.

All have sinned and fall short of the glory of God. Everyone born is born a sinner and is thus unrighteous. Everyone's heart is wicked. Because God restrains sin and bestows good gifts, that wickedness is revealed or veiled in varying degrees. Whereas some persons may appear especially wicked while others distinctly good, their hearts are afflicted with the same condition, for there is in truth no distinction. Common grace is like the insulin pumped into my body to keep my diabetes under control so that I appear to be healthy. It does not heal my disease.

If then we lie under the verdict of being unrighteous and are deserving of judgment, if we are unable to justify ourselves or to work ourselves out of our predicament, what can we do? The answer is nothing. Only God can do the necessary work to make us righteous and to bring us out of condemnation. And he did it. He put forward Christ Jesus as a propitiation—that is, as a sacrifice that satisfied the required judgment for our sins. He made propitiation by shedding his blood—by dying—on the cross. By that propitiation we were redeemed from our sins—their guilt and their penalty. And we even obtained righteousness through faith in Jesus Christ and his work. Not only did he take the guilt and penalty of our sins, he transferred to us the status of righteousness so that we might appear before God justified. It is not a righteousness of our own that we demonstrate every day, but a righteousness of Christ. To summarize, we are sinners separated from God and under his judgment. Out of his mercy this same God provided a solution to our problem by sending his Son to die on our behalf. If we will believe on this same Son, Jesus Christ, we will be justified.

How then does understanding this doctrine—Christ's work on the cross—simplify what common grace tends to obscure?

First, it makes clear the state of the unregenerate heart. We do not need to apply some kind of spiritual thermometer to know the condition of the heart that has not received the atoning work of Jesus Christ by faith. The heart is not merely sick; it is dead in trespasses and sins (Eph. 2:1).

The simple question for us to ask ourselves whenever we feel that a person ought to be accepted as good enough or religious enough is, what was the cross for? I addressed this more fully in my chapter on the good neighbor. Suffice it to restate that if a person could be good enough to be let into heaven, why would God the Father send his Son to die a bloody death? Looking to the cross should be the cold water splashed on our faces to awaken us back to reality. The sinful condition of the heart is real. The biblical statements about righteous deeds being filthy rags (Isa. 64:6 KJV) and about no one being righteous (Rom. 3:10) are not extreme statements made to frighten us. They are divine diagnoses of the unregenerate heart. Why else the cross?

We don't need to argue with anyone over his relative goodness or lack thereof in order to diagnose his heart. We need merely to look to the cross for what it teaches about the human heart. If so great a person (the Son of God) was needed to make the sacrifice for our atonement, if such a costly sacrifice (his precious blood) needed to be made for our ransom, how great our sinful condition must be.

Christ's work on the cross simplifies our understanding of his holiness and righteousness. We cannot plumb the depths of such mysteries, but we can at least toss aside the shallow concept of God as a nice grandfatherly figure who is willing to overlook our indiscretions. The cross shows us a righteous, holy God who must remain true to his character. It shows a God who is not like us in our sinful frailty. We need not debate whether God is just, especially in comparison with us. We simply need to look to the cross to know that sin cannot exist in the presence of such holiness.

Finally, Christ's work on the cross brings clarity to the matter of God's mercy and love. However much anyone may assert that a merciful God would overlook sin, no one would be willing or able to take the extreme measure that God undertook to be both just and the justifier. It is God who sees clearly the depravity of the human heart. It is God who cannot tolerate such pollution. It is the same God who pays the supreme price of offering up his own Son for . . . his children? No. His friends? No. He did it for his enemies (see Rom. 5:6–10). Now that is mercy and love.

The mercy and love displayed in common grace is wondrous. Even then, what baffles both the regenerate and the unregenerate alike is the seemingly random dispersion of that grace. And no matter what anyone receives, they would still like to have a little bit more.

There is no variance in the measure of special grace—the grace enacted on the cross and then applied to the heart to bring about redemption. We may be surprised by who receives it, but there is no receiving a little amount of it while others receive a greater amount, as in the case of common grace. Every one of the redeemed receives the "riches of his glorious inheritance in the saints" (Eph. 1:18).

That we are in rich in Christ allows us to welcome the generosity that our heavenly Father shows to the unregenerate. How can we begrudge temporal blessings when we have before us "an inheritance that is imperishable, undefiled, and unfading, kept in heaven for [us]" (1 Peter 1:4)? Why would we question the kindness of common grace shown to the ungrateful and the evil when we, who once were the ungrateful and the evil, received the saving kindness of special grace? Special grace puts common grace in perspective.

Whether the grace of God is the special grace of redemption or the common grace of providence, it is grace unmerited that springs from the kind heart of our heavenly Father. By grace our Creator created us; by grace he restrained his just wrath when our parents failed. By grace our Provider continued to sustain, even to bless, the world. By grace our Father sent his only begotten Son, full of grace and truth, to save us on the cross as our Redeemer. By grace he sent his Holy Spirit to give us faith unto salvation. And by grace he will receive us unto himself on the last day.

For Discussion

1. What is the answer to how we account for good in people whom Scripture declares to be unrighteous?

2. How should the concept of common grace keep us humble?

3. What is the simple motivation that common grace teaches for loving the unregenerate and for working for good in our communities and societies? Who is our model?

4. What are the limits of common grace?

5. What is the critical difference between common grace and special grace?

6. What are the dangers of common grace?

7. How do we protect ourselves from these dangers?

8. How does the redemptive work of Christ simplify what common grace can obscure?

9. How does special grace put common grace into perspective? How should it keep us from begrudging the common grace shown to the unregenerate?

Notes

Foreword

1. James Davison Hunter, *To Change the World: The Irony, Tragedy, and Possibility of Christianity in the Late Modern World* (Oxford: Oxford University Press, 2010), 232.

Acknowledgments

1. *De gemeene gratie* (Leiden, Netherlands: D. Donner, 1902).

2. Ed. Jordan J. Ballor and Stephen J. Grabill, trans. Nelson D. Kloosterman (Grand Rapids: Christian's Library Press, 2011).

3. From *The Princeton Theological Review* 7, no. 3 (1909): 437–65.

4. Phillipsburg, NJ: P&R Publishing, 1972.

5. Edinburgh, UK: Banner of Truth, 1991.

6. Sermon, All Saints Presbyterian Church, Richmond, VA, January, 1989, available online at http://storage.cloversites.com/redeemer presbyterianchurch3/documents/ComGrace.pdf.

7. Grand Rapids: Eerdmans, 2002.

Introduction: The Problem of Good

1. Quoted in *Prose and Poetry of England*, ed. Julian L. Maline and Wilfred M. Mallon (Syracuse, NY: L. W. Singer, 1949), 434.

2. William Walsham How, 1864; text of 1875.

3. John Calvin, *Institutes of the Christian Religion*, trans. Ford Lewis Battles, ed. John T. McNeill (Philadelphia: Westminster, 1960), 273–75 (2.2.15).

4. Ibid., 275.

5. John Murray, "Common Grace," *The Collected Writings of John Murray* (Carlisle, PA: Banner of Truth, 1977), 2:92.

Chapter One: Restraining Sin and Wrath

1. For a further discussion of the identity of these "daughters" and the "sons of God," read Victor P. Hamilton, *The New International*

Commentary on the Old Testament: The Book of Genesis, Chapters 1–17 (Grand Rapids: Eerdmans, 1990), 261–65.

Chapter Two: My Father's World: The Good Gifts of Common Grace

1. John Murray, "Common Grace," *The Collected Writings of John Murray* (Carlisle, PA: Banner of Truth, 1977), 2:102.

2. John Calvin, *Institutes of the Christian Religion*, trans. Ford Lewis Battles, ed. John T. McNeill (Philadelphia: Westminster, 1960), 180 (1.14.20).

3. Albert M. Wolters, *Creation Regained: Biblical Basics for a Reformational Worldview*, 2nd ed. (Grand Rapids: Eerdmans, 2005), 24–27.

4. Calvin, *Institutes of the Christian Religion*, 180 (1.14.21).

5. See ibid., 273 (2.2.14).

6. Abraham Kuyper, *Wisdom and Wonder: Common Grace in Science and Art*, trans. Nelson Kloosterman (Grand Rapids: Christian Library, 2011), 35.

7. Calvin, *Institutes of the Christian Religion*, 274–75 (2.2.15).

8. Ibid., 273–75 (2.2.16).

9. Westminster Confession of Faith 16.3.

10. See Calvin, *Institutes of the Christian Religion*, 293–94 (2.3.4).

11. Murray, "Common Grace," 113.

12. See Richard J. Mouw, *When the Kings Come Marching In: Isaiah and the New Jerusalem*, rev. ed. (Grand Rapids: Eerdmans, 2002).

Chapter Three: Worshiping and Glorifying the Creator and Provider

1. Folliott S. Pierpoint, "For the Beauty of the Earth," 1864.

2. Joseph Scriven, "What a Friend We Have in Jesus," 1855.

Chapter Five: Common Grace and Loving Your Neighbor

1. Trevin K. Wax, *Holy Subversion: Allegiance to Christ in an Age of Rivals* (Wheaton, IL: Crossway, 2010), 145–46.

2. *Contra Faustum*, book 17, trans. Richard Stothert, *Nicene and Post-Nicene Fathers, First Series*, vol. 4., ed. Philip Schaff (Buffalo: Christian Literature Publishing Co., 1887), rev. and ed. Kevin Knight, *New Advent*, 2009, http://www.newadvent.org/fathers/140617.htm.

3. "Prepare Me One Body," African American spiritual.

4. John Wilbur Chapman, "Jesus! What a Friend for Sinners," 1910.

5. C. H. Spurgeon, "Fire, Fire, Fire," *The Metropolitan Tabernacle Pulpit* (Pasadena, TX: Pilgrim Publications, 1969), 7:396.

Chapter Six: How Should We Then Live in the World?
1. C. S. Lewis, *Mere Christianity* (1952; repr., Nashville: Broadman & Holman, 1980), 179–82.

2. John Calvin, *Institutes of the Christian Religion*, trans. Ford Lewis Battles, ed. John T. McNeill (Philadelphia: Westminster, 1960), 252 (2.3.4).

3. John Murray, "Common Grace," *The Collected Writings of John Murray*, vol. 2, *Systematic Theology* (Carlisle, PA: Banner of Truth, 1997), 93.

4. Ibid., 102.

5. Thanks to David Thompson for insights into these issues. Thompson to Skeel, email, October 2, 2012.

6. Hauerwas has often made this point in the context of calling the church to model a truly biblical community. See, for example, Stanley Hauerwas, *A Community of Character* (Notre Dame: Notre Dame Press, 1981).

7. See Amartya Sen, *Development as Freedom* (New York: Alfred A. Knopf, 1999); Peter Singer, *Practical Ethics*, 3rd ed. (New York: Cambridge University Press, 2011).

8. See Sen, *Development as Freedom*.

9. The B Corp website, which explains the benefit corporation concept, can be found at http://www.bcorporation.net/.

10. Richard J. Mouw, *When the Kings Come Marching In: Isaiah and the New Jerusalem*, rev. ed. (Grand Rapids: Eerdmans, 2002). See, for example, page 40 on this point.

Chapter Seven: How May We Learn from the World?
1. St. Augustine, *On Christian Doctrine*, trans. J. F. Shaw, in *Nicene and Post-Nicene Fathers*, ed. Philip Schaff (Peabody, MA: Hendrickson, 1999), 2:545.

2. Ibid.

3. I am dependent for this information on the notes in *The ESV Study Bible* (Wheaton, IL: Crossway Books, 2008), 2122.

4. J. Rendel Harris, "St. Paul and the Epimenides," *The Expositor* 8, no. 4 (1912), 352. This is the last in a series of three articles Harris

wrote on the subject. Harris pieces together fragments, draws on quotations from other ancient authors, and documents his discovery of new sources. He reconstructs the text based on an abundance of textual and extratextual evidence. Together the articles constitute a *tour de force* of "old school" biblical and classical scholarship. See also his "The Cretans Always Liars," *The Expositor* 7, no. 2 (1906), 305–17; and "A Further Note on the Cretans," *The Expositor* 7, no. 16 (1907), 332–37.

5. See Harris, "The Cretans Always Liars," 307–10, 314–15.

6. See William H. Pahlka, *St. Augustine's Meter and George Herbert's Will* (Kent, OH: Kent State University Press, 1987).

7. See Gustav Wingren, *Luther on Vocation* (Eugene, OR: Wipf & Stock, 2004). See also Gene Edward Veith, *God at Work: Your Christian Vocation in All of Life* (Wheaton, IL: Crossway, 2002).

8. See G. K. Chesterton, "The Paradoxes of Christianity," *Orthodoxy* (Garden City, NY: Doubleday, 1959).

9. T. S. Eliot, "Metaphysical Poetry," *Selected Prose*, ed. Frank Kermode (New York: Harvest, 1975), 59–67.

10. Ibid., 64.

11. For a more complete account of this approach to secular learning see Gene Edward Veith, *Loving God with All Your Mind: Thinking as a Christian in the Postmodern World* (Wheaton, IL: Crossway, 2003).

Chapter Nine: The "Good" Neighbor

1. *The Temple*, 5th ed. (Cambridge: T. Buck and R. Daniel, 1638), 183.

2. Thomas Kelly, "Stricken, Smitten, and Afflicted," 1804.

3. Elizabeth Studenroth (unpublished poem, used by permission).

Conclusion: The Limits of Common Grace

1. John Calvin, *Institutes of the Christian Religion*, trans. Ford Lewis Battles, ed. John T. McNeill (Philadelphia: Westminster, 1960), 277–78 (2.2.18).

Contributors

D. Marion Clark (M.Div., Gordon-Conwell Theological Seminary) served as executive minister of Tenth Presbyterian Church in Philadelphia. He has edited two devotionals derived from the sermons and writings of James Montgomery Boice: *To The Glory of God* and *Come to the Waters*. He also contributed the chapter "Baptism: Joyful Sign of the Gospel" to *Give Praise to God: A Vision for Reforming Worship*.

Ruth Naomi Floyd (A.A., Art Institute of Philadelphia) is a vocalist and composer who has been at the forefront of creating vocal jazz settings that express Christian theology. Ruth leads her own multifaceted ensemble, and her discography consists primarily of original compositions. She is a noted fine art photographer specializing in black and white archival images. She has long been involved in compassion ministry to individuals with HIV/AIDS, and she serves the transgendered community. She teaches music at The City School in Philadelphia and at Cairn University in Langhorne, Pennsylvania.

Steven J. Lawson (Th.M., Dallas Theological Seminary; D.Min., Reformed Theological Seminary) is president of OnePassion Ministries, a ministry designed to bring about biblical reformation in the church today. He is the professor of preaching for The Master's Seminary and he oversees the Doctor of Ministry program there. He is also professor in residence for Truth Remains. Dr. Lawson is the author of twenty books, the most recent being *The Evangelistic Zeal of George Whitefield*.

165

John S. Leonard (M.Div., Reformed Theological Seminary; Ph.D., Trinity Evangelical Divinity School is pastor of Cresheim Valley Church (PCA), which he started in the Mt. Airy / Chestnut Hill section of Philadelphia. Previously he served as associate professor of practical theology at Westminster Theological Seminary and as a missionary under Mission to the World and Arab World Ministries. His recent book is *Get Real: Sharing Your Everyday Faith Every Day.*

Sean Michael Lucas (M.A., Bob Jones University; Ph.D., Westminster Theological Seminary) is senior minister at First Presbyterian Church in Hattiesburg, Mississippi. Previously he served as chief academic officer and associate professor of church history at Covenant Theological Seminary in St. Louis. He is coeditor with D. G. Hart of the American Reformed Biography series and editor of the Basics of the Faith series (both with P&R Publishing). Among his many books is *God's Grand Design: The Theological Vision of Jonathan Edwards* (2011).

David Skeel (J.D., University of Virginia) is professor of corporate law at the University of Pennsylvania. Skeel writes on bankruptcy and corporate law as well as on sovereign debt, Christianity and law, and poetry and the law. He is a contributor to a number of publications, including the *Wall Street Journal* and *Books and Culture*, and has been interviewed on *The News Hour*, *National Public Radio*, and *Marketplace*. His most recent book is *True Paradox: How Christianity Makes Sense of Our Complex World* (2014).

Paul David Tripp (M.Div., Reformed Episcopal Theological Seminary; D.Min., Westminster Theological Seminary) is president of Paul Tripp Ministries, through which he works to connect the transforming power of Jesus Christ to everyday life. An international conference speaker and author, he speaks and writes on a variety of practical subjects for Christians and pastors. His most recent books are *Sex and Money: Pleasures That Leave You Empty and Grace That Satisfies* and *Dangerous Calling: Confronting the Unique Challenges of Pastoral Ministry.*

Gene Edward Veith (M.A., Ph.D., University of Kansas) is provost and professor of literature at Patrick Henry College. Previously he served as professor of English at Concordia University in Wisconsin and as culture editor of *WORLD* magazine. He has contributed widely to articles, reviews, and papers on Christianity and culture. He is the author of more than twenty books, and his most recent publication is *Family Vocation: God's Calling in Marriage, Parenting, and Childhood.*